Praise for Lisa Priest's previous book, *Conspiracy of Silence*

"AN ALMOST UNBELIEVABLE STORY . . . A COMPELLING READ with its combination of true crime, fascinating characters, newsworthiness, mystery, scandal, and a good solid story." – *The Vancouver Sun*

"A TAUT, READABLE rendition of the awful facts." – *Winnipeg Free Press*

"A thorough job, fairly presented." – *Books in Canada*

"The story, combined with Priest's painstaking research, make **Conspiracy of Silence** A WORTHWHILE READ." – *Halifax Daily News*

"A nasty tale of racial prejudice taken to the extreme ... It is hoped Priest's book will wake people up to the fact that sensitivity toward and genuine tolerance ... of native and ethnic minorities are long overdue." – *The Ottawa Citizen*

D1736981

ALSO BY LISA PRIEST

Conspiracy of Silence (1989)

LISA PRIEST

Women Who Killed

*Stories of Canadian
Female Murderers*

M&S

An M&S Paperback from
McClelland & Stewart Inc.
The Canadian Publishers

An M&S Paperback Original from
McClelland and Stewart Inc.
First printing May 1992

Copyright © 1992 by Lisa Priest

Canadian Cataloguing in Publication Data

Priest, Lisa, 1964-
Women who killed

ISBN 0-7710-7153-1

1. Women murderers – Canada – Biography.
2. Murderers – Canada – Biography.

HV6535.C3P7 1992   364.1'523'092271   C92-093707-1

Cover photographs (top to bottom): Elouise Roads Wilson
(Ralph Bower/*Vancouver Sun*); Agathe Brochu; Micheline
Poulos (Pierre Coté/*Canapress*); Harriet Giesecke;
Cheryl Lynn Tutty (*Canapress*)

Photograph of Robert and Irene Pearson cannot be
reproduced in any form without the express written
consent of the publisher.

Typesetting by M&S, Toronto
Printed and bound in Canada

McClelland & Stewart Inc.
The Canadian Publishers
481 University Avenue
Toronto, Ontario
M5G 2E9

Contents

Acknowledgements

This book is a collection of 11 stories about Canadian women who have killed for love, children, money, or freedom from abuse. Some slayings were done accidentally in the heat of passion while others were coolly planned and carried out with the precision of an assassin. And then there are Cheryl Tutty, Lisa MacDonald, and Mae Favell who didn't mean to hurt anyone at all.

This book draws from interviews with police officers who investigated these women, the Crown Attorneys who prosecuted them, lawyers who defended them, and the psychologists and psychiatrists who assessed them for the purposes of testifying in court. And then there are those such as Irene Pearson, whose lives are forever shattered when someone they love is slain. Thousands of pages of trial transcripts, documents filed in court and the memories of credible sources formed the basis of my research. This book took me to Montreal, Vancouver,

Halifax, Kingston's Prison for Women, and Windsor.

Several of the subjects allowed themselves to be interviewed for this book. I would like to thank Harriet Giesecke, serving time for the first-degree killing of her estranged husband; Mae Favell who was recently released after knifing her common-law husband Ernie Pelly; Khristine Linklater who had the courage to turn her life around, and Elouise Wilson, who is on parole after serving time for second-degree murder.

I would also like to thank a number of others who helped me in my research. A very special thanks goes to Dennis Curtis of Corrections Canada and his staff. Wayne Frechette, Bruno Cavion, Bob Morris, Rupert Ross, Serge Côté, and Hazel Blythe were all of great assistance. Defence lawyers John Rosen, Joel Pink, Robert Sachitelle, James and Alix Sutherland, and Hersh Wolch gave me every assistance consistent with the requirements of duty to their clients. Thanks to psychologist Luc Granger, and psychiatrists Peter Rowsell and Edwin Rosenberg. Thanks to Glenn Stannard of Windsor Police, Neale Tweedy and Wayne Oldham of the Metropolitan Toronto Police Force, and Julian Fantino of London Police Force. I have also received help from a number of others who would prefer me to not thank them by name.

Thanks to my literary agent and staunchest advocate Helen Heller and her partner, another good friend, Daphne Hart. Thanks to my editor, James Adams of McClelland & Stewart, who believed in this project and his assistant, Trish Lyon. A special thanks goes to Brian

McAndrew, and other editors at *The Toronto Star* who were always supportive and willing to accommodate me when I needed time off to write.

My sister, Barbara, was of continual support to me as was my father, Arthur Bernard Priest, who continued his lifelong encouragement, even as he was dying of cancer.

Introduction

Historically, women killers have been the subject of ridicule. They have been portrayed as bosomy, pouty-lipped double-agents lusting for men one moment, killing them coldly the next. They have been labelled freaks, demons, and the deadlier species. Even a woman writer, F. Tennyson Jesse, said in her 1924 book *Murder and Its Motives* that the female murderer "is the panther of the underworld. She can follow relentlessly through the jungle day after day, she can wait her time, she can play with her victim and torture him in sheer wantonness, and she can pile cruelty upon the act of killing as does the panther, but never the lion."

Those statements couldn't be further from the truth. Homicides by women are exceedingly rare and more frequently are the result of one woman's desperate attempt to rid herself of an abusive man. Unlike men, who are apt to kill a total stranger in a bar during a drunken brawl,

women tend to kill their cheating lovers, violent husbands, and unwanted newborn babes. In short, women
kill those they have *loved*.

Despite this fact, women killers have not been taken
seriously. They are either the subject of grimly amusing
anecdotes or they are analyzed in terms of their disorders. In fact, they should be studied in the society in
which they live, with special attention paid to that society's public policies. What makes one woman in horrendous circumstances kill, when another woman will find a
more peaceable way out? What pushes one woman to
plan a killing for a baby while others will simply allow the
courts to do its job?

In her book, *Women Who Kill,* Ann Jones writes: "The
undeniable fact is that women — and I'm speaking now
of all women everywhere in the world at every period of
recorded history — hardly ever kill anybody." She further states that "if one were to count killings in military
combat as homicides, the percentage of killing done by
women worldwide would shrink out of sight."

Statistics support Jones' claim. In Canada, women are
responsible for 15 per cent of murders, attempted murders, assaults, sexual offences, robberies, and abduc-
tions. In 1990, 89 females were charged with homicides
across the country, according to the Canadian Centre for
Justice Statistics, whose figures are the most recently
available. Of those, 27 were charged with first-degree
murder, making the incidence of first-degree murder 1
per 100,000 women. Men, however, still commit the vast
majority of crimes. One out of 100 women are charged
with crimes, compared to seven for every 100 men.

History has shown us that murder by women occurs in the most ordinary of circumstances. The poet Enid Bagnold wrote that "a murderess is only an ordinary woman in a temper." As flip as that epigrammatic statement sounds, Bagnold may have been onto something. Pushed past that line of tolerance, any one of us could submit to the ultimate human explosion.

Take the life of Mae Favell, a native Indian living in northern Ontario, the opening chapter of this book. One doctor called her the most battered woman he had ever seen. Indeed, the abuse she sustained from her husband of 16 years was horrendous. She had been burned with cigarette butts, had an axe swung at her genitals, and a wine bottle shoved up her vagina. She called police 16 times in one year to report the assaults, yet they continued. Police were of the thinking that she was giving as many licks as she was getting. Her impulse to fight back seemed to *lessen* the culpability of her husband's behaviour. The beatings only ended when Mae stabbed her husband to death. Yet Mae was judged as an individual manifesting abnormal behaviour, instead of being seen as someone caught in a relationship of domination and subordination, a power struggle over life.

A similar situation occurred in Halifax when Lisa Melva MacDonald knifed her common-law husband, ending a very destructive relationship. Beaten and sexually abused, MacDonald was the one, according to her sister, who couldn't handle stress. The killing was looked at in terms of *her* behaviour. Macdonald was repeatedly beaten, cheated on, and controlled by a man who earned her trust as a brother-in-law when she was a child and then abused it by becoming her lover. Yet she, alone, was the one with the problem.

One of the most heart-wrenching stories in this book is that of Cheryl Tutty, a Catholic university student, who became pregnant out of wedlock for the second time. She was a young woman who wanted a career in her immediate future, not a family. Alone, she gave birth rapidly and suddenly in a bus toilet. Thinking the baby was dead, she left it there and went back to school. She was charged with second-degree murder and after the judge said there wasn't enough evidence to go to trial, the Nova Scotia attorney general's department took the very unusual move of bringing the case back when it preferred a bill of indictment. The father of her child testified against her. Those in the east coast were reeling about what a horrid woman *she* was, while the father of the child was left unscathed, unjudged.

Beatrix Campbell aptly stated: "The woman who kills is exactly what she is supposed *not* to be. Her act is deemed not only unnatural but impossible in a real woman; so she is 'unwomaned' by her violence and as this classic aberration, exiled from her community and her gender." Indeed, women have long been stereotyped as givers of life, rather than takers, peacemakers rather than warriors. But whether they are strong, weak, dependent, independent, submissive, or dominant, women, ultimately, are the authors of their own acts, as you will read in these 11 chapters.

While researching this book, I met with several of the women killers, the most moving and complex of whom is

Harriet Giesecke. Extremely manipulative, Giesecke is university-educated, articulate, and ruthless. Desperate to gain custody of her baby, she planned the murder of her estranged husband, Randall Giesecke. Of all the killers I have interviewed – men or women – Giesecke stands out as the most deliberate. Although she has never admitted to killing her estranged husband, evidence revealed that she desperately wanted Randall Giesecke dead and was willing to do anything to achieve her goal.

There are other "genuine" killers in this book, what those in P4W (Kingston's Prison for Women) call the real murderers. They are dark characters who disturb and fascinate. They disturb because they plan their killings down to the last grisly detail. They fascinate because murder in itself is so final, so irrevocable. It is the human equation that I find riveting. What pushed lawyer Elouise Wilson to strangle her ailing cousin for money? Why did Adele Gruenke beat an old man to death for an inheritance? And what made Agathe Brochu think she could get away with planning the murder of her stingy husband? Thousands of women live in these circumstances. They want, or feel they deserve more money while others yearn to rid themselves of their dullard husbands. Some fail to change their circumstances because they are scared, lazy, or have learned to be long-suffering, figuring it is their lot in life. Others go crazy. Many find a suitable solution, usually by divorcing.

The women in this book, however, felt there was only one way out – with a gun, knife, or a piece of twine – and they took it.

ONE

"I Think I Killed Him This Time"

SHE awoke with the most incredible hangover that November morning. The pounding sensation was matched only by the one she used to get when her husband kicked her in the head with his steel-toed boots. A dry, cotton mouth and a queasy stomach made Mae Favell feel like curling into a fetal position and sleeping off the pain. But first, she wanted to find out where her common-law husband, Ernest Pelly, was. Looking around, she realized she was in a jail cell.

A woman whom Mae didn't know was walking along the corridor of the lockup at the Vermilion Bay detachment of the Ontario Provincial Police (OPP). Mae caught her eye through the cell bars. Was Ernie Pelly in the next cell, she asked. Mae figured they must have been picked up on "drunk warrants" again.

The woman looked at her, shook her head in disbelief, and trudged along without a word. Mae was perplexed. It seemed like a simple enough question.

What 52-year-old Mae didn't remember – nor does she to this day – was that she had stabbed her husband in the groin with a knife so hard and so deep that he bled to death in their two-room cabin. She also doesn't remember going to her former husband John Favell's home to tell him she thought she killed Ernie just a few minutes before OPP officers arrived at her home that November 21, 1985.

When officers turned up at 6:45 p.m. that November 21, Pelly, 42, was indeed dead. Lying in a pool of blood on the log-cabin floor was a small, pitiful man who, had he been alive, might not have been sober enough to tell the story of how he got in such a sorry state. More often than not, Pelly was drunk from morning until night. So intoxicated, in fact, that he and Mae didn't always know the time of day, the date or much of anything else other than the fact that they seemed to hate each other with all their might.

OPP constable Rod Case was one of the first officers to arrive at the scene. The two-room cabin was cloaked in blackness. When he arrived, Ernie was sprawled out on the floor. An incredibly inebriated Mae was nearby. Case pushed up his cap, pulled out his notepad, and scribbled down his thoughts. "I could tell right off the bat he [Ernie] was done," Case said later in an interview.

As Case looked at the scene, Mae crawled on the floor, babbling at her dead husband. She tugged at his bleeding body saying "Ernie baby" and "what's wrong with Ernie" and "I love Ernie." The old man had been nicknamed "Pin Cushion" by his male friends because of the constant beatings he sustained at the hands of his common-law wife. But Mae's female friends in town knew differently. Ernie started the attacks. Ernie's death was no surprise to Case or anyone else in the fishing village of 680 located about 90 km east of Kenora, near the Manitoba border. The police had been frequently dispatched to the couple's home. Neighbours, fed up with hearing shrieks, screaming, and the breaking of furniture often would call the officers to get the pair to stop their noisy violence. Mae would also call officers if she felt matters were getting too out of hand.

Although the police frequently answered these domestic disputes, they didn't lay charges. That's partly because police felt the couple wouldn't show up for court, said Case. Moreover, police didn't see this as a classic case of "battered wife syndrome" because "Mae used to whop the shit out of him all the time. They would fight and scream and bash each other and everybody was in love five minutes after that. They never ever spent any time apart. They were always together." Police were of the opinion that Mae was giving more licks than she was getting. At one point, she sliced off part of Ernie's ear during an argument. No one – not even Mae – knows why they fought so much. They blamed it on the alcohol.

This violence took place in a part of northwestern Ontario that the tourism industry calls Sunset Country. Vermilion Bay, a mostly white area, is located on the crossroads of Eagle Lake and Red Lake and boasts one fly-in and seven drive-in lodges. Some of the best walleye, northern pike, bass, muskie, sauger, yellow perch,

and lake trout fishing can be found in the tiny village that
features a six-day "Walleye Willy" fishing derby in the
summer.

Despite the postcard-perfect scenery, Mae and Ernie
lived a life that belied this natural beauty. There was talk
that once upon a time in their 16-year relationship, Mae
and Ernie had gotten along. But you would be hard-
pressed to find many who remember anything other than
their week-long binges and vicious fights. There was
always a new cut, another black eye, a bash to her
already-bashed in face. Often, Mae, a once-attractive
woman, would be so wasted from a night of drinking and
damage that she wouldn't bother to wash the blood out of
her hair the next morning. It would stick together, matted in clumps. Seemingly indifferent, she'd sit in a diner,
talking between her sips of coffee about anything and
everything except last night's brawl.

At first, people in Vermilion Bay expressed wonder-
ment at the volatile pair. "I could never understand it,"
said Thomas Favell, 47, a nephew of Mae's. "They both
seemed to satisfy themselves beating one another."
Townsfolk, too, were bewildered by Mae's tolerance for
pain. But after a while the quizzical stopped trying to figure out the bizarre.

When sober, Mae and Ernie were likeable. Some
would even say kind. Townsfolk were willing to talk to
the pair, provided they weren't under the influence.
Geraldine Harrison, then 55, often opened – and then
closed – her door if one or the two of them came to her
place bombed. "I gave up drinking, I don't need that

trouble," she said in an interview. Getting a whiff of their rye-laced breath was enough to know that a volcano of emotions was about to erupt. And no one wanted to witness that.

It was no wonder then that one of them got killed. How long could the ever-escalating abuse last? "He'd beat her up and then she'd beat him up," said the nephew. "I guess it was more or less inevitable that one of them would end up dead."

Dead right. Ernie's demise pitted the Pelly family against the Favells and soon the bitterness soured Vermilion Bay. The Pelly family said Mae provoked the whole mess. "You might say she instigated it," Arnold Pelly, 35, told the *Winnipeg Free Press*. "Ernie was the weak defenceless one – he was always drunk."

There's little doubt that Mae got her swipes in. At the same time, she had suffered extensive physical and sexual abuse at her husband's hands. And when Dr. Alan Torrie of the Lake of the Woods District Hospital in Kenora evaluated her for defence lawyer, Greg Brodsky, he was shocked with what he found. "She was the most battered woman I had ever seen that was alive. I suggested she get corrective surgery."

There were some things – things too excruciatingly painful – that Mae just couldn't bring herself to tell Dr. Torrie. It was embarrassing, sitting in the doctor's office, trying to detail all those horrible incidents. And how could she remember them all, anyway?

One event did remain crystal clear in her memory, though. It was the time the pair got tanked on cheap wine, went home and got ready for bed. Mae put on her nightgown and was ready to retire for the night. She snuggled in and started to snooze. "The next thing I knew I was hurting like hell," she said at her trial. "I woke up and saw him standing there with a bottle of Cold Duck. Blood was trickling down my leg from my vagina. I told him he was sick."

Another time, Ernie, in another of his wild drunken rages, swung an axe at Mae's genitals, slicing her clitoris. "I couldn't move and it got real sore and started swelling," Mae said later. With every step, the pain grew more intense. The sharp jabs were interspersed with gnawing agony. Mae didn't know if she could make it out the door to get advice and aid from her family, many of whom lived in Vermilion Bay and in Ear Falls, another fishing village 95 km to the north.

When she finally did make it out of the house and over to her relatives, they said she should report Pelly to the police. However, Mae declined: if Pelly were taken into custody, he'd lose income from his seasonal jobs as a kitchen hand, pulp and paper worker, and wild rice picker. "I showed it to my family and they said I should report it, but I didn't because he'd only miss work."

Mae never sought medical attention for any of her injuries because she said there were no doctors available and there was no way for her to travel to see one. Scars covered her body in bumpy layers. The right wrist healed in a disfigured manner, her left was broken, her face resembled that of a mashed piece of pulp rather than the well-defined Ojibwa features she had been blessed with. Her nose, once a distinct, attractive feature, was now crooked and lumpy. It had been broken three times, obstructing her right nasal passage. Long, thin scars zig-zagged across her head. "They're so numerous I can't tell which is which," she said later, parting her hair to show the jury at her trial.

The wounds multiplied over the years and there were no holidays from abuse. During the summer, the pair would go up north to a remote bush camp where they would work splitting wood. Sometimes, they would get jobs at a tourist camp at Separation Lake, located about 50 km northwest of Vermilion Bay. When they weren't working, they would collect unemployment insurance.

The fights at the bush camp were as abusive and pain-ful as all the others. Pelly once smashed a 26-ounce sherry bottle across Mae's face, cutting open the top por-tion of her lip. "My lip was just hanging down and my teeth were showing through." Three teeth fell out. Even-tually, the lip healed with the uneven curl of a potato chip.

Another time, the pair were picking wild rice together when Ernie suddenly lunged at her. "All of a sudden he gives me two kicks in my back and threw me to the ground. He held me down and put his hands around my throat. I started to see black spots and heard a humming in my ears. I grabbed him (by the testicles) and held on. Then he leaned over and bit my nose. I still have the teeth marks."

Sometimes Ernie would stomp and kick Mae in the face with his steel-toed boots. Sometimes he'd take a lit cigarette and stick it into her arm. Burns were on both arms, three on her back, one under her chin, two on her waist, one on her stomach, two more on her legs. "He got so crazy drunk and did it while I was passed out," she said in court. "I woke up and saw him doing it. The pain of the burning woke me up when he was making the deepest one."

Why did she put up with it? Why does any woman? "I loved him. He was the father of my kid and I thought he'd change," she replied. In court, Mae testified that she called the Vermilion Bay OPP detachment 16 times in 1984-85 to report incidents. "One time he started kicking me around and said he'd kill me by setting me on fire. He had such an insane look on his face. I called the police and the constable said: 'Oh yeah, I heard he had served time in Stony Mountain, [a medium-security penitentiary near Winnipeg, Man.] for arson. Just chase him away.'"

In fact, Ernie did have an extensive criminal record spanning the years 1962 to 1976. He had been charged with various assaults, break and enters, mischief, and failing to appear, with most of the offences taking place in Dryden and Red Lake, Ont. He was charged with arson in 1970. Even people in town weren't that crazy about him. "I would have never trusted him for anything," Thomas Favell said later. "He was a well-known thief. Drunk or sober, he'd steal the shirt off your back." Other people thought he was the nicest guy around and commented how he wanted to be everybody's buddy when he was drunk.

For some, it seemed, the only order Mae Favell could handle in her life was complete disarray. Having been raised in a household where violence was commonplace, she knew nothing else. Initially, she didn't take the abuse her common-law husband handed out. She would punch, hit, throw things at Ernie to stop him from hurting her. Sometimes she would even start the blow-ups herself, and they wouldn't always be with Ernie. Geraldine Harrison, who has known Mae since she was 16, remembers receiving a frantic phone call from her mother, Evelyn Huusko, who lived up on the hill in Vermilion Bay. In a weak, broken voice, Huusko, a woman in her sixties, said something about getting "beaten up." Harrison didn't wait for the rest of the story. She hung up the phone, put on her shoes and raced out of the house to her mother's small-frame home, located several steps up the hill from the Favell–Pelly residence.

Harrison arrived panting to find her mother "was getting beat up by Mae. I didn't give her a chance to explain, I told her to get out."

Mae fled the house and Geraldine stayed with her shaken mother. It wasn't the first time Huusko was a victim of the couple's antics. Harrison supplied her mother with groceries, wood for the stove, and other household amenities. She checked on her daily, trying to provide her with the basics of a quiet, peaceful life. But peace is one thing Huusko didn't get: Mae and Ernie occasionally would break into her home and ransack her refrigerator for groceries. "What little she had is what they took," Harrison said. "Mae was mean when she was drunk."

Mae Favell was one of those unfortunate thousands of natives who grew up in a world where her native culture had been stripped away and substituted with a so-called higher way of thinking – the white man's way. If she spoke Ojibwa at residential school, she, like her brother and sister, was chastised. She was brought up to study English and Christianity, to erase from her mind the customs and traditions of her own culture or be punished if she did not. "Anybody who has been in a residential school has had a tough life," Thomas Favell says. "And Mae was no different."

The raw facts of native life in Canada are frightening. About 500,000 Canadians are listed as status Indians by the federal government, giving them the right to live on remote reserves with no resources, no jobs, no independence. If they are lucky, there might be plumbing but most natives tend to live in homes that are overcrowded, without central heating or indoor toilets. Native people are four times as likely as the rest of Canadians to die from violence or poisoning.

Native youth are five times as likely to commit suicide and infants are more like twice as likely to die before they are one year old. While some argue that native alcoholism is no greater a problem than non-native alcoholism many Indian leaders single it out as a devastating vice for its people. Out of such circumstances came one Mae Favell.

"Most of our family were heavy drinkers and developed alcoholism at a young age. I know I did," Thomas says. "Back in those days everybody drank." Mae's parents separated when she was young. By the time she was

16 or 17, she married John Favell, who was about the same age. They had their first child, a boy, Clarence, almost immediately. Six more children followed over a 15-year period; Vivian, Carol, John Jr., Dorothy, Valerie and Lisa.

Mae was strict and harsh when controlling her children. "I thought she used to be rough with her children – in disciplining her kids," Thomas says. "She used to hit them – particularly Clarence. She used to hit him pretty hard."

Sometimes, Mae would pick up Clarence by the "scruff of the neck and throw him halfway across the room." Having children in her teens and well into her twenties, Mae felt trapped. She had missed that carefree period of life when the only responsibility was to yourself. Soon, though, her children grew up and began having children of their own but it wasn't long before tragedy struck.

In 1976, Clarence was at a party in Vermilion Bay when he suddenly hit the floor: he had been shot in the back and the wound paralyzed him from the waist down.

"There was a fight at the party and Clarence was walking out the door when he was shot," Thomas Favell recalls. The injury "made him very bitter and angry at the whole world." Clarence tried to make the best of his circumstances. After all, he was a married man with two children, so there was more than just himself to worry about. But with his role as father, husband and lover diminished, "I think he became impotent and that affected him dramatically." At the age of 27 Clarence had

had enough. He fired a rifle into his mouth and thrust two families into heart-wrenching despair.

Mae, who had been separated from her first husband, John, since 1968, was especially devastated. Clarence's death became the subject of sad, whimpering stories told over innumerable beers consumed at fleabag bars and all-night parties. It was forever the excuse for her to drink herself into a stupor. Meanwhile, Ernie, whom Mae had taken up with a year after she left her husband, proceeded to get more abusive. As the years passed, pain became routine and death a palpable possibility. Mae must have thought of death as a welcome relief to her suffering.

What exactly happened the night of November 21, 1985, is something Mae still tries to recall. "I don't remember Ernie being stabbed. Whether I did it or not, I don't know." All she knew was that the emotional torture and baggage had to be dumped somewhere. After she was charged with manslaughter she was released on bail and ordered to attend Clarissa Manor, a 14-bed alcoholism treatment centre in Kenora, where she met Doris Horne, the director.

Doris, 50, knew probably better than anyone else what abuse was. She had been beaten and subjected to sexual abuse. She knew just how hard those memories were to shake. In fact, this mother of six was smart enough to know they couldn't be. They had to be worked out, "placed in a drawer," and said goodbye to.

It took Horne many years to finally be free of her

painful circumstances and, after working at the Kenora Detox Centre from 1971 to 1981 as an attendant, then as a shift supervisor, she landed a job as a counsellor at 208 Water Street, a makeshift hostel for women in trouble. There, she immediately saw that women needed something more – they needed a treatment centre. Doris and others in the community gathered exhaustive statistics on wife abuse, alcoholism and drug problems to show the government the need for such a centre. After all, men had a home for drug and alcohol recovery in Kenora. After the centre, known as Clarissa Manor, was approved, Horne applied for the job of director and was there for its April, 1986 opening. Today, the provincially funded shelter serves residents throughout northwestern Ontario and Manitoba.

Doris Horne knew all about alcoholism – the stuff that numbs the next beating. She had spent years of her marriage getting drunk so the beltings wouldn't hurt as much as when she was sober. She knew what it was like to feel she wasn't worth anything. Nothing shocked this woman. The only exception was when Mae Favell came to the recovery unit while waiting for her trial. "She had this haunted look about her," Doris remembered. "She was really a broken down lady."

An optimist, Doris believed Mae could recover and have a life. She needed only to look at her own past life to see that miracles can happen. Doris had made a tremendous recovery and turned all her hurt into useful experience to help heal those who needed her most. Mae Favell was one of her "projects."

Mae blamed herself. Although she couldn't remember

killing Ernie, she believed she did. At the same time, she couldn't understand why and she mourned for him constantly. "There were many nights when she didn't sleep," Doris said. "It was really sad. She couldn't handle being alone."

Horne and Favell commiserated together. They swapped stories of abuse, talking deep into the night, early into the morning. This camaraderie helped Mae. She needed to hear the voice of experience. They talked of a "bottle courage," of the punch packed in liquor that would numb them, and help them forget, ever so briefly, the horrible beatings.

What Mae had to face was the prospect of spending the rest of her life in jail. Conviction on a charge of manslaughter can mean a life sentence. Doris Horne was convinced Mae had acted in self-defence. But would a jury? Mae's presence, although scarred and bruised, was also substantial. She was big-boned and tomboyish, and looked like a lady who could take care of herself. Would the scars, burns, and broken bones be enough proof that she had lived with a sick, perverted man in a kill-or-be-killed relationship?

The case against Favell was solid. Police had the murder weapon, a knife with a 15-cm blade, found buried in a woodpile next to her home, and a confession of sorts to her former husband. Besides, Mae wasn't about to deny she killed Ernie – she just couldn't remember doing it.

At the preliminary hearing on March 5, 1986, Mae's former husband John, who was also a cousin of the victim, testified that he was drinking with the pair the day of the killing. At 3:45 p.m. that day, Ernie purchased four bottles of cheap sherry and asked Mae's former husband to join them. John said yes and went to the two-room cabin where he drank about four tumbler-size glasses of wine. An argument broke out at 5:15 when Mae, jealous of Ernie, started to accuse him of "screwing around" with another Vermilion Bay woman. Knowing how violent the pair could get, John made a quick exit. The last words he heard while shutting the kitchen door were: "You're screwing Patsy Hill."

About an hour later, Mae came over to John Favell's home and asked to borrow a couple of cassette tapes. Despite the cold temperatures, she wasn't wearing a jacket. "While I was getting them from the bedroom she says 'I think I killed him this time.'" John looked at her. "She said 'We got another bottle over there if you want another drink.'" As they walked out the door, Mae said, "You're not going to like what you're going to see over there."

John locked his door while Mae kept walking, about 90 metres ahead of him. As she reached her street, she waved her arms to a neighbour across from her home. "She was trying to tell me something and I just went like this and took the snowblower and kept going with it. I proceeded to do what I was doing." Moments later, he saw John Favell running down the street after Mae. When John reached the cabin, he saw Ernie on the floor next to the couch, lying in his own blood. John took two strides toward him and touched him underneath the chin for a pulse, something he remembered from his St. John ambulance training. He ran to a neighbour's home and telephoned the police.

A post-mortem report revealed that Ernie died from a loss of blood. The stab wound in the left femoral artery, a long vessel that runs from the thigh and down the leg, would not necessarily have been fatal if prompt medical attention had been given. Crown attorney Rupert Ross said later in an interview, "This cut in Ernie's leg would have needed three stitches. The problem was that everybody was too pissed to get medical attention." The post-mortem also revealed that Ernie's blood-alcohol level was almost four times the legal level of impairment.

Dorothy Dawe, 26, testified that she had lived with her mother, Mae, and stepfather, Ernie, in their rented cabin since 1982. There is only one door inside the house, which leads to the kitchen. The other room in the cabin is the bedroom. Early on the day of the killing, a few neighbours had come over with a dozen tiny bottles of liquor. Everyone was getting intoxicated that morning so Dorothy decided she didn't want to hang around anymore and boarded a bus for Ear Falls.

The pair never fought when they were sober, she said. But they did when they were drunk and her mother frequently had black eyes and bruises. They drank "until it was all gone or they passed out." The neighbour with the snowblower said he had seen the pair in some real knock-down, drag-out fights. "I've seen them many times beating each other up and drunk and falling down and in fact there was a few times I had called the police over there because we were trying to have a barbecue out in the back yard and they were swearing and drinking."

Ernie, he said, was more of a pain than anything. "Ernie was a pest, you know, like the neighbour's dog always coming over, you know, and you give him a sandwich and the dog comes back the next day. Well, that's like Ernie pretty well." He had seen Ernie take a baseball bat to Mae and figured she was going to get beaten to death. "All of a sudden, it seemed to me like it was a wrestling game. Mae got up and she says to Ernie 'give me that.' He handed her the baseball bat and the next thing Ernie was on the ground … And the last I seen Mae had her blouse ripped open, they were both bleeding and they were going up the trail and one said to the other one 'Oh, I'm sorry I hit you so hard. I didn't mean to you know but you make me mad' and they were in love, they were gone. It was a normal thing to me."

Shortly after midnight on November 22, 1985, two officers saw Mae in the lock-up. When the officers told her she was being charged with murder, she was stunned. "Murder, murder, murder," she murmured. Officers asked if she knew what that meant and she replied, "Yeah, woah, murder." After being read her rights, she said she wanted to make a statement but officers didn't get very far during the interview because she couldn't remember anything.

"Holy shit, Jesus Christ" she kept repeating. Finally, in a moment of utter despair, she yelled, "Jesus Christ, oh Lord. Tell me what did I do?"

"Why did you take that drink?" Mae said ruefully to herself. "See what that one drink led to."

Mae asked how she did it and they told her Ernie had been stabbed. "The last thing I remember we went to the liquor store and he went and got John Favell for a few drinks. Johnny left and I went to get a few tapes. Let's have a drink before you go back. I had a bottle hidden where I keep my cribbage board. God be with him and me. I don't remember bugger all." Her mind, she said, was a complete blank. She didn't even recall the jealous argument over Patsy Hill.

Her thoughts now were focused on how she was going to live alone. "Ernie, Jesus Christ I love you," she cried as tears streamed down her face. Too upset to talk anymore, she was led back to her cell.

With the trial set for early September, Greg Brodsky, a prominent Winnipeg lawyer, was hired as Mae's defence counsel. Noted for his successful defence of Victoria Savoyard, Brodsky has earned a reputation as a top-notch criminal lawyer. He argued that the 35-year-old Savoyard, who endured 10 years of beatings from her common-law husband, suffered from "battered wife syndrome." She was trapped in a world so horrible she could find only one way out – with the blade of a knife – and she took it on January 27, 1985. She was charged with manslaughter for the death of John McDonald in the hamlet of Minaki, located a short drive north of Kenora. Throughout the trial in April, 1986, the six-woman, six-man Ontario Supreme Court jury heard how Savoyard had endured a history of beatings through her on-again, off-again relationship with McDonald. Broken bones, bruises and cuts were the battle scars she had sustained in their marriage. Yet, she always went back to him and got beaten again.

As McDonald kicked her in the back on January 27,

she picked up a butcher knife, turned around, and saw blood. The pathology report determined McDonald died of a pierced lung.

Madame Justice Mabel Van Camp told the jury there was no question Savoyard stabbed McDonald. "What isn't admitted is whether it was an unlawful act or criminal negligence." Savoyard's state of mind was a crucial question to the jury. In a precedent-setting verdict on May 1, 1986, Victoria Savoyard was acquitted of John McDonald's death.

Four months later, Brodsky, a tenacious trial lawyer, adopted a similar defence strategy when he faced Ontario Supreme Court Judge Wilfred Dupont in the same Kenora courtroom that hosted the Savoyard trial. Mae didn't — nor could she — deny killing Ernie. The best Mae, now 53, could hope for was the judge's sympathy to the horrible abuse she sustained. In September, 1986, the jury accepted her plea of guilty to manslaughter.

After her plea, she took the stand to tell of the monotonous routine of vicious beatings. Her testimony was complemented by the unbuttoning of shirts, the parting of hair and rolling up of pantlegs to show what havoc one person could wreak.

Brodsky cross-examined his client. He needed to present a sympathetic picture and he did. While arguing for probation instead of a jail sentence, he looked directly at the jurors and said: "I don't know how lucky *you* could be to survive that long. With being hit over the head with bottles, hit with axes, being stabbed and having a bottle put up her vagina, she still survived ... In addition to beating her, he used her in the most gross ways. It not only demonstrated what he thought of her, but what she was prepared to accept. She does not need to go to jail. Nothing would be accomplished by her incarceration."

Crown attorney Rupert Ross, who worked as a fishing guide for 12 years in Minaki before becoming a lawyer, had a hard time asking that Mae be incarcerated. This case was far removed from the years he spent in an aluminum boat with an open motor, taking guests through the cold Ontario waters and cooking them up deep-fried pickerel, northern pike and bass on the shore.

During sentencing, Ross asked that Mae Favell be given a six-month incarceration. It would, he suggested, send out a message that the courts treat domestic violence as they do other type of violence. "I told the judge I can feel Mae Favell's eyes on my back and I hate having to ask for this because she's been a victim all her life," he said in an interview. "What we had was two out-of-control people with too many histories of sorrows and griefs and pains."

At sentencing, Ross said, "What Mrs. Favell went through is nothing short of ... I can't find the appropriate word for it. The question is, can the court deal with this? Domestic violence must be treated like all other forms of violence. It must be dealt with as a crime. Your Lordship must send a signal to the community of how domestic violence will be treated by the courts. It's not a position I like to be in, but as Crown, this must be dealt with severely by the courts ... A period of incarceration wouldn't place a hardship on Mae Favell that life couldn't continue for her after."

After that submission, Brodsky jumped to his feet. He was determined to not leave Mae Favell behind steel bars. "You don't know, nor does anyone, how that wound came to be on the deceased or the bruising Mae had when she woke up in jail ... She called the police 16 times in the last year to complain of the deceased abusing her and they said: 'Kick him out' ... The police aren't exactly divorced from the Crown."

On September 19, Justice Dupont told the lawyers he needed several days to consider the evidence and Mae's testimony. He returned to the courtroom five days later. He said he accepted the fact that Mae was too intoxicated to remember killing Ernie, pointing to testimony which showed she drank what would normally be considered a lethal volume of alcohol on November 21, 1985. "There are many other assaults which the court won't go into, but the fact is that they have left Mae Favell with a scarred mouth, wrist and arm, misshapen ears, broken teeth and numerous other scars," Dupont said. "Her relationship with Pelly has reduced her to a less than complete individual. To have the punishment inflicted on her and accept it put her on a subhuman level without any rights. There will be no jail sentence." Instead, Mae Favell would be placed on three years probation. While Dupont said he agreed with the thrust of the Crown's submission, he said he still could not jail her since she posed no threat to the community and was cooperating fully with her alcohol treatment.

By contrast, the dead man's brother, Arnold Pelly, expressed disgust with Mae's release, calling it grossly unfair. "I think she should have been given time for that crime. Three years probation – it makes it look like the man's life was worthless." The Pelly family, which included himself, another brother and three sisters, didn't follow Favell's trial because they wanted to "put this thing behind us. The family has always been aware that he wasn't the one doing the beating. Ernie was the weak defenceless one – he was always drunk," he told reporters.

Ross, too, also thought the sentence belittled the man's life and he didn't see it as the classic case of the "battered wife syndrome" because "she wasn't a prisoner in the relationship. It's a social and cultural cataclysm put together with poverty and alcohol."

Women's groups hailed the judge's decision. Doris Horne and Charlotte Holm, a spokeswoman for Women's Place, a Kenora crisis line for battered women, said they were pleased. "For the second time this year, the battered wives' syndrome has been successfully used to defend women who have been abused," Holm said, citing the Savoyard acquittal. "It's a tragedy when people die like this. But people can only take so much."

Mae Favell, relieved by the sentence, burst into tears. "I was surprised," she said quietly to reporters. She said she was afraid she might be sent to jail. "Now, I'm pretty happy." Justice had been served. It was time to get on with a new life, which included working at a Kenora hotel and receiving treatment.

Mae's life is finally quiet. There are no fights, no boozing, no one to sap what strength she has. And she needs that strength more than ever. At the time of this writing,

Mae Favell was fighting for her life once again, having been hospitalized on and off for multiple myeloma, a form of blood cancer. It may turn out to be the biggest fight of her life.

TWO

More Than Friends

A BITTER northwesterly wind made the cold January afternoon seem even colder. But inside his modest Winnipeg apartment, Philip Barnett wasn't thinking about the weather.

Sitting in the living room, he was busy flipping through one hot photograph after another of naked women. He wanted to make love to each and every one of them, their ripe, lusting bodies awaiting the pleasure that only a man, it seemed, could give them.

At least that was Barnett's fantasy. It had been a long time since he had actually made love. And now, at age 81, he sensed such carnal knowledge was going to be harder and harder to come by.

Only a few weeks before, in December, 1984, his wife had died from complications related to alcoholism. Barnett had been good to her. He had cared for her, he defended her against the tenants who gave them an awful

time with their noisiness and frequent confrontations.
Now he wanted something for himself and glossy photos
of nude women were hardly a satisfying substitute.

Other than a few nieces farther west and two brothers,
including one who lived in Montreal, Barnett had no
immediate family living in Winnipeg. He and his wife
didn't have children. For the first time, he was faced with
the prospect of dying alone. The only way he could cope
was by wanting so desperately to live. He had accomplished what most people set out to. He had had a long
marriage, homes, cars, and a career as a manufacturers
agent that had earned him a sizeable income. What he
lacked was what he felt was life's greatest pleasure, sex.

Barnett's desire had become a full-blown obsession
after his wife's death and he started to ogle women as they
walked down the street. In anticipation of the day when,
hopefully, fantasy would become reality, he kept himself
in shape, shovelling snow from the sidewalks, walking up
and down the steps to his third-floor apartment every
day. Agile, alert and vibrant, he easily passed for a man in
his sixties.

One woman whose looks appealed to him was his
landlady, Kate Ford. Sometimes while she cleaned the
laundry room he hung off her shoulder and asked for a
little kiss on the cheek and a hug. He hoped these ges-
tures would start something but Ford only waved him off
like a pesky garden bug.

Realizing that "straight sex" might not be in his
future, Barnett offered a compromise. Would Ford consider giving him a spanking? That would give him

enough of a rush. Ford declined. "I always treated it as a bit of a joke. I said, 'No thank you but thanks for the offer anyway.' He said he would make it worth my while but I still declined."

While in his room that cold January in 1985, Barnett read a copy of the *Winnipeg Sun*, a daily tabloid. An article by gossip columnist Maureen Scurfield caught his attention. It was about a massage technique known as reflexology, and how a licensed masseuse, Adele Rosemarie Gruenke, one month away from her 21st birthday, was offering the technique. A photo of Gruenke accompanied the article. Barnett thought she looked attractive and his thoughts now wandered to massage parlours and visions of well-endowed women rubbing him with warm oil. For a fee, they might even do more, he prayed. Could these reflexology treatments be the same type of thing? Determined to find out, he clipped the article and called La Femme Total in River Heights, a prestigious area of the medium-sized prairie city, to make an appointment.

Over the telephone, Adele Gruenke explained that reflexology was a type of preventative therapy. Using pressure points on the foot, it helps the body heal itself. Gruenke had entered the business at 19 or 20 – she couldn't remember when – after seeing a masseur for a back injury she had sustained in a car accident.

When Barnett arrived for his session, he mumbled something about a troubled hip. He and the tall, pretty brunette went into a back room for treatment. Much to his chagrin, he discovered that reflexology really did involve using the pressure points of his feet. There were no chesty girls, no stroking of private parts. Still, Gruenke seemed like a lovely young woman. They talked for a while.

A depressed Barnett told Gruenke how his wife had died recently from the ravages of alcohol. While he didn't want to get into all of the details, he indicated his marriage had been unsatisfactory. It was the first time in a long while that Barnett actually felt himself opening up.

Gruenke had also suffered a terrible loss. Just one year earlier, her father had died after a long, torturous bout of leukemia. Chemotherapy hadn't helped and now Gruenke, who always felt estranged from her father, was without the very man she had longed to be close to. Regrettably, she didn't say the things she had wanted during his five-year sickness. Now she was resentful, hurt, and without faith in modern medicine.

Adele Gruenke was born on February 20, 1964 to Michael and Joanna in North Kildonan, a pretty area of north Winnipeg. A sister for Eric and Rudy, she was the only natural child of Michael Gruenke, Joanna's second husband. The carpenter had adopted the two young sons when he married Joanna, a hairdresser. A pretty girl, Gruenke was frequently the centre of attention in her family and among friends at River East Collegiate and she relished this as she got older. In her late teens, she posed for photographs, hoping to make the cut for Miss Park Pontiac, doing print and television promotions for the popular car dealership. She never lacked for boyfriends during her teens and spent part of her leisure time caring for a horse she owned at Birds Hill Park stables.

Although generally "laughing and bubbly," she was prone occasionally to "being grouchy and a bear," according to her brother, Rudy. You had to be careful not to provoke her because "she could get a temper."

Although all the Gruenkes lived together, there were distances between them and when Michael Gruenke took ill in 1980, things fell apart. Joanna, for one, became extremely anxious, Rudy remembered. "For the last year or so he was gradually fading away – we were going back and forth to the hospital."

The last week of Michael Gruenke's life was the worst. "He couldn't recognize anybody. He didn't know me or anybody," Rudy said. "It was really hard on Adele." Michael Gruenke was not even 55 years old.

Her father's death made young Adele vulnerable. It was while floating adrift in a sea of loss, with seemingly nowhere to turn and no one to comfort her, that she met Phil Barnett. It was the beginning of what appeared to be a father/daughter relationship. With almost 60 years between them, it could also have easily been a great-grandfather/great-granddaughter relationship.

Barnett started to visit La Femme Total every week for treatments, involving a jumbo vibrator, cream, reflex-ology "guns" and Gruenke's hands – all of which were used on his feet. He frequently came to these sessions with flowers and chocolates in hand. Sometimes the pair went for a bagel and a coffee and talked. He seemed interested in her career. He wanted to help and she seemed to like that.

Within weeks, the gifts became more elaborate and expensive. A $500 leather dress, scuba diving gear with an accompanying course at University of Manitoba, a coat, and jewelry. Then there were trips – to Expo '86 in Vancouver and to Los Angeles. He even bought her a brand-new Chrysler Laser. And there could be more, Barnett promised. He could help Gruenke by setting her up in her own salon. Indeed, Barnett gave her $1,700 to set her up as a masseuse at Paolo's Hairstyling, located in an affluent section of Winnipeg. A close friend of hers, James Robert Fosty, then 24 and an apprentice at Canadian National Railway, helped with some of the carpentry work for her section of the salon. There was no shortage of men willing to help out. And she wasn't shy to take advantage.

Eleven months after their first encounter, Adele Gruenke and Phil Barnett had moved in together. They had purchased an $89,000 home in one of Winnipeg's more fashionable subdivisions. Gruenke's mother — who had given her daughter $15,000 for the downpayment; Barnett had provided the rest — was concerned about the arrangement, but Gruenke assured her that she and Barnett were merely friends. They would have separate bedrooms. It was a housemate relationship, she explained, not a love interest.

Gruenke settled into the home and continued to spend lots of time with Barnett. They watched television, went out for dinner, and took in the occasional movie. She did the grocery shopping and cared for him. It seemed a most accommodating relationship.

After moving in, Barnett got credit cards for her and

she used them willingly. Pantyhose, lingerie, boots, shoes, blouses, makeup – she bought them all. But her eagerness to be the "material girl" seemed to cloud what a street-smart woman should have known all along – that Barnett was no amiable, asexual "sugar daddy." He wanted a lot more than just lighthearted chatter.

It didn't take Barnett long to make his intentions known. One evening he broke down and begged Adele to let him suck her toes. Shocked and reluctant, Adele declined at first but then, worn down by his persistent pleading, she relented. Seeing the old man at her feet, however, made her feel "awkward." That's as far as he got with her.

Within a month of moving in together, Gruenke went on a two-week ski trip with friends. Barnett didn't seem to mind but on Valentine's Day a jealous streak began to show. James Fosty gave Gruenke a "Snoopy" Valentine's card and a "wee little bottle of perfume." Barnett noticed it sitting on her dresser. Heated words were exchanged. A week later, Gruenke and Barnett were having a birthday dinner at her mother's house when Gruenke mentioned that Fosty had bought her a stuffed koala bear. Barnett started moaning about how Fosty meant more to her than he did. "I couldn't get across to him that Jim and I were just friends and the gift didn't mean anything."

Shortly thereafter, Gruenke noticed that none of her friends seemed to call her at the home she shared with Barnett. She'd place messages but no one returned them. It wasn't until several of her friends asked why she hadn't been calling that it clicked in. Their messages were being left with Barnett who wasn't passing them on. He wanted Gruenke all to himself. He also was snooping through her bedroom, rifling through her personal letters, including one from a man in Los Angeles.

Clearly, things weren't working out as Phil Barnett had hoped. Adele Gruenke wasn't so filled with gratitude at his generosity that she wanted to throw her naked body on top of him. Time was important because he didn't have a lot of it. And because young Adele was the only "prospect" he had, he pursued it with all his might.

Gruenke, meanwhile, continued with her objectives, which seemed to involve taking the old man for as much as possible. Near the end of February, she learned of a highly recommended college in Boulder, Colo., that taught naturopathic therapy classes. She and Barnett discussed the 15-month course, which started in the fall, and how it would be beneficial to her career. Gruenke applied, was accepted, and talked with Barnett about closing the shop at Paolo's.

In early April, she landed a job at Birds Hill Park where she worked as a trail guide. One month later she met a pleasant young man named Garth Andrew Carmen Davisson who later became her boyfriend. He worked as a tour guide, horse trainer and general maintenance man at the riding stables. She told Davisson about her father/daughter relationship with Barnett, and how he had purchased expensive clothing and a car for her. Davisson didn't put too much credence in it.

Gruenke complained to Davisson that Barnett was a jealous man and hated seeing her spend time with her friends. She told him she just wanted to escape. Davisson noticed that Adele was becoming increasingly sullen, wan and listless. Well, she finally explained, I think I have leukemia. By the end of May, Adele Gruenke did appear to have lost considerable weight and often complained of feeling sick. Finding it difficult to work, she moved in with her mother in June in North Kildonan.

Barnett was upset. He wanted to take care of her, not her mother. They had "hot words" as she moved out. "He was accusing me of doing things, of sneaking around. I just wasn't comfortable there." As she walked into her bedroom, he said "that I wasn't just going to walk away scot free and think that I could just – that I could just walk out of his life and think that this was the end." Barnett, in fact, vowed to take "drastic measures" if she ever obtained a boyfriend. Gruenke then called her mother and told her to reach James Fosty to tell him to pick her and her things up. By nightfall, everything was out of the Charleswood house. Gruenke was relieved.

It didn't take long before Barnett came back, apologetic. "I think it was after the weekend and he said he was really sorry and he was crying and he begged me to come back and he was telling me how much he missed me and that he didn't really mean all of those terrible things he said." Gruenke, however, was having none of it. She told her former roommate that she would never, ever live with him again.

Over the past few months, she had lost 15 kg. Instead of her usual, healthy 64 kg figure on a medium, tall frame, she looked slight and sickly. On a recommendation from a friend, she decided to go to Portland, Ore. to get tested for four or five days at the Sunnyside Health Center and Chiropractic Clinic, a place that tests people "naturally." Davisson agreed to accompany her. Specialists there recommended she go on a very extensive vitamin program – something that would cost hundreds of dollars a month. They did determine, however, that she did not have leukemia as she had feared. (In late September, 1986, she would tell Davisson she had been lying the whole time and, in fact, did not have leukemia, according to Davisson.)

Returning to Winnipeg in August, she began to talk to Barnett again. She told him about the expensive vitamin therapy the Oregon specialists had recommended. He offered to pay her $250 a week for the regime.

In October, Barnett flew into a rage when Gruenke told him she and Davisson had just broken up. Barnett hadn't known they were lovers – he just thought they were workmates. Discovering the true nature of their involvement made him livid. "If you can put out for Davisson, you can certainly put out for me. I have spent so much money and time on you, I should get something in return. You owe me some kind of love."

Gruenke was shocked by this and told him so. Then she got angry. "The more persistent he got, the sicker I became because I just couldn't handle this," she said. "I thought of this person as someone who was helping me, not trying to destroy me. I told him that the more he persisted, the sicker I became. I would just think about this and I would get myself really sick."

In November, Barnett went over to the Gruenke house to see Adele, who was ill in bed. "I had gotten out of bed to talk to him and he said that he felt that I was healthy enough to come across and he didn't really want to discuss it because my brother had just come home so he just said, you know, 'Make sure you are at my house tomorrow at 1 o'clock.'"

Gruenke then called James Fosty to tell him what Barnett was up to. She was disgusted and sickened by the entire scenario. "I told him what Phil had expected of me that afternoon and I said, there's no way I can go over there and degrade myself like that."

Fosty told her not to go. Gruenke called Barnett to say she was too sick to visit. "You're stalling," he said. Adele shot back that she really was ill and that his badgering was worsening her illness. Barnett then told her to "catch a few winks" and to call back at about 4 o'clock.

"I called Phil back and he insisted that he see me that night [November 28, 1986] and he made it very clear that I best be in the frame of mind to come across," she said. Upset, she again called Fosty who said she was "going to have to face the music." Was is really that hard, he asked, to tell an old man she didn't live with to get lost?

That evening, wearing black tights, a white pullover with splashes of color, black high heels and a black jacket with a fur collar, Gruenke stepped out to meet with Phil Barnett in an apparent attempt to talk. She carried an evening purse, with a rhinestone clasp. Adele Rosemarie Gruenke was dressed to kill.

At 9:30 p.m. Vic Black was driving his tow truck down Highway 405, also known as River Road. He'd just finished hauling a truck from Winnipeg to Lorette, 15 km south of the Manitoba capital, when a cream-coloured car caught his eye.

The car, a late-model Ford Tempo sedan, was parked in the ditch. Strange, Black thought as he backed his truck up to shine his headlights onto the rear of the car. The lights revealed nothing. Black wondered what the hell this car was doing in the ditch. Sure, it was cold out – at least minus 8° C – but the highway wasn't slippery, so how could it have skidded off the roadway?

On closer inspection, Block thought he saw a person inside but he wasn't sure. Concerned, he tapped on the frost-covered windows but no one responded. He tried to open the driver's door but it was locked.

There were two possibilities, Black thought. Either the driver had had one drink too many and decided to sleep it off, or perhaps someone had left their hockey equipment in the car and locked it up. Still, a cold Black didn't really want to stick around too long to find out. Thinking there was nothing wrong, he left.

Two hours later, Robert Porteous was driving south on that same stretch of highway when he noticed the same Tempo still in the ditch. He kept on his course but about a kilometre later, he had this nagging feeling something was wrong. He turned around and headed back to the Ford. Like Black, Porteus pulled up behind it and shone his headlights on the car. Unable to see anything, he stepped out of his car and looked inside but the frost-coated windows made it tough to see. Porteus finally found a clean patch of glass. "I looked inside. Then what I seen to be a body. I went back to my car, went home, told my parents about it. My mom called the police."

Slumped in the passenger's seat was an old man swaddled in blood-stained clothing. His skull was bashed-in, frozen chunks and flecks of which were pasted on the windows and interior. RCMP officers from the nearby St. Pierre detachment were summoned to the scene, which they cordoned off. The Mounties began a door-to-door canvass of neighbours to try to find out if they had seen anything suspicious. Identification officers photographed footprints and tire tracks.

RCMP Sergeant Howard Kearley, a Mountie for 27 years, arrived at the scene shortly before midnight. He noticed that the Tempo sedan had veered gently off the highway and travelled about 50 metres through snow before it came to rest. He quickly surmised that the car had not swerved off the roadway but had been purposely driven in that way.

He noted "… it was an elderly white male sitting in a basic upright position with his head slumped slightly forward on the chest, that there were massive, ghastly, ragged, open-type wounds in the area of the right temple."

Blood was all over the man's face, head, parka and pants. Skull fragments were found on the front seat, floor boards, upholstery, even underneath the gas pedal.

Early the next morning, at a farmhouse three km east

from the scene, Shirley Dawn Chechvala placed a call to police. The night before she had driven home from a hockey practice with her children when she noticed a toque in the driveway of her home on Highway 207. At first she thought nothing of it and tossed it on a shelf in her garage.

It wasn't until morning that she grew concerned. The light allowed her to see what she couldn't before – congealing blood packed in snow at the foot of her driveway. There, officers also were to find crunched bone fragments partially frozen in the ice and snow, a broken, brown plastic rim from a pair of eyeglasses, a tooth, and hair.

About 2.2 km west of the murder scene, strewn along the south shoulder of the highway, police found sixty-six slides, featuring pictures of a woman in her mid-20s. "They were just strewn – strewn there with no particular pattern," RCMP constable Clifford Ellis Russell would testify later. "Some areas would have two to three within a space of 3 metres. Other places would be one individual slide."

In the meantime, in Winnipeg, police had gone through the victim's pockets, where they found a wallet with money and credit cards. They quickly dismissed robbery as a motive. On the driver's licence was the name Phil Barnett. There was $99 and change, keys and various miscellaneous bills and cards. And one other thing – Adele Gruenke's business card.

Once police had the man's identification, an officer went to his apartment at 525 Lanark Street in Winnipeg

– the same place Barnett's wife had died – to search for clues to the killer and a name for next of kin. The first thing RCMP Corp. Jim Brown noticed was how clean the suite was. He scanned the rooms, noticing a newspaper on the kitchen table. He walked over to find a tightly folded copy of the November 28 *Winnipeg Free Press*. He surmised that Barnett likely had picked up his newspaper on the way out for the night and placed it on the kitchen table.

Within a few minutes, Brown had found an index card with relatives names on it and, interestingly enough, a folded will, lying on the top of Barnett's dresser.

Dated July 18, 1986, it read:

"In the event of my death, I, Philip Barnett, being of sound mind and body leave the interest on the amount of my estate to Adele Gruenke presently residing at 214 Stuart Avenue, Winnipeg, Manitoba for as long as she lives and any material possessions should be sold and money realized of any assets invested with the balance of my assets.

On the death of the said Adele R. Gruenke my estate will be divided equally among the following, Mrs. Susan Truffa, Ms. Elizabeth Barnett, Ms. Peggy Barnett and Ms. Margaret Palmer, St. George Anglican Church.

Should Adele Gruenke pre-decease me, paragraph 2 will come into effect. P. Barnett."

Just four months after penning these words, Barnett was dead. How convenient, Brown mused. Was the old man killed for his money? Brown was determined to find out.

Meanwhile, Manitoba's chief medical examiner, Dr. Peter Markesteyn, had determined that Barnett had died of extensive head injuries as a result of blunt trauma. In layman's terms, the victim had been beaten to death with a dull instrument. Other than coronary artery disease, and some hardening of the arteries, the medical examiner concluded the victim was in "a reasonable state of health" before the time of his death.

On November 29, Sgt. James Bernard Bell of Winnipeg Police went to tell Adele Gruenke that her former housemate was dead. She asked how and he told her it was by "violent means." He asked if she might want to shed some light on the incident, downtown at the Winnipeg Police station. She agreed. Fosty joined them later.

On the drive to the station, Gruenke was not shy about discussing her involvement with the old man. She freely admitted that she and Barnett had lived together for a time. In fact, his will, she said, named her as "executor," although she didn't seem to understand what exactly that entailed. The money was left to her, she explained, because his two brothers were over 65 and they didn't need it.

"How much money has Phil spent on you since you met him?"

"A lot," Gruenke replied.

"How much?"

"I don't know for sure. Quite a bit. I never tallied it up. My car was $12,800. He bought me a lot of clothes. I couldn't even begin to tally up. He wrote me cheques at $250 each, every other week. He gave me $1,500 to help me get out of debt when I first met him. He gave me $1,100 this past summer to go to Expo, Portland, Oregon, and Los Angeles, California."

When the officer suggested that surely their relationship was more than father-daughter, Gruenke replied: "Why would I want to get rid of someone who pays all my bills?"

At the police station, James Fosty told interrogators that on the day of the murder, he had picked up Gruenke, gone gift shopping at a mall, paid a visit to the Nor-Villa Hotel, then dropped her off at her mother's house before returning home to get ready for a night out.

Later, Adele and James went to a coin-operated wash to clean his 1986 Grand Am, did more shopping, went to a bar where they played pool and then out for a pizza, he said.

Clearly, Adele Gruenke was the single, strongest suspect in the case. Her situation was the stuff of old mystery novels: a huge will is written by an old man and left to a young, attractive woman. The plots don't get anymore predictable than that. Had Barnett been able to choose his voyage to the Almighty, though, it would have been between the thighs of a young, willing woman. At least then he could have exited with a smile on his face.

While at the police station, Gruenke drafted a handwritten, five-page statement outlining her friendship with Barnett and her activities the night of his death. Since Gruenke's story about November 28 was essentially the same as Fosty's, police had to determine if it stood up or not.

A visit to the Nor-Villa Hotel proved fruitful. Shayne Bolin, a carpenter and doorman there, told officers a regular by the name of Jim Fosty came to the hotel November 28 around 3 or 4 p.m. In recent days, Bolin had been pestering Fosty for a nailpuller, (a long, slender tool with large steel teeth on the end) and he asked Fosty when he could purchase it. Fosty told him it was no problem. He was going home for a shower and change and he would bring it back later. Between 7:30 and 8:30 p.m., Fosty turned up with the nailpuller in hand for which Bolin gave him $10. Police seized the tool and discovered it had traces of blood on its shaft.

One person who had a special interest in the killing was counsellor Janine Frovich of Winnipeg's Victorious Faith Centre, a 200-member born-again Christian church. She had counselled Adele Gruenke previously, after meeting her at the church. As soon as she heard of the murder from a friend, her thoughts flashed to her former parishioner. Gruenke had first come to Frovich in the fall of 1986 when Gruenke was convinced she was dying of leukemia. She had also complained to Frovich that she was having "a lot of problems" with Phil Barnett.

"She wanted more of a daughter-father relationship and he was more or less demanding a lover relationship and she really didn't want to go through with that," Frovich would testify later. "And, she mentioned that he was helping her financially and that she really needed that and she also confessed to me that she was thinking of murdering him, and I didn't take her too seriously at the time."

Gruenke saw Frovich for about four weeks, then, in late October, the masseuse determined that she was "healed" and she didn't need any more help. "She was feeling good and she was looking much better," Frovich said. "Phil had been coming to church off and on with her. She seemed happier. She didn't seem to have, she told me didn't have those recurring thoughts of murder, so I felt comfortable with that."

Gruenke visited Frovich one more time after this to tell her that Garth Andrew Davisson had dumped her after six months of going steady. He said he didn't love her anymore. In addition, she told Frovich that Barnett was putting the heat on her again. He wanted more time with her. Alone. Preferably naked.

When Frovich learned the old man had died, she "put two and two together." A message from God told her that Adele Rosemarie Gruenke was the killer. "After I received that one phone call about Phil's death, I questioned it within myself and I feel that God did confirm an inner gut feeling that she had done it."

Two days after the murder, Frovich contacted Gruenke by phone. "I asked her if she would like Bill (Frovich's husband) and I to go over and talk to her because she said she was really feeling guilty and she was very upset." Bill and Janine went to Gruenke's house but because Gruenke found it too difficult to talk there, the three returned to the Frovich residence. "Adele approached me about, what if someone had committed murder, could God forgive that. And, what if someone had committed murder, would they go to hell," Frovich said. After a few of these "what ifs" Frovich asked Gruenke what she was trying to say. Gruenke started to weep. "I killed Phil," she blurted.

Frovich tried to console her. If Gruenke repented before God, she said, she would be forgiven and would not have to go to Hell. She related the Bible story of how Israel's King David had taken another man's wife and sent her soldier husband into combat to be killed. Even though David had repented, he still had to face the consequence of sin, which was the loss of his firstborn, Absalom. "I approached her about telling the truth. I was saying to her in order to be set free you must tell the truth, not only before God but before man," she said. "I explained to her that she not only committed a sin before God, but she commited a sin before man. She broke man's law."

Knowing the job was too big for her, Frovich called pastor Harmony Thiessen and explained what happened. The trio arranged to meet at the church that evening. It was a tense, 30-minute drive. Once they arrived, Gruenke asked Frovich if she still would have taken her into her home, knowing what she'd done. "I said that I had loved her, that I had known she had done it and that it was okay," Frovich said later.

When Pastor Thiessen walked into her office, she saw a seemingly deeply grieving Gruenke and a tearful Frovich rubbing Gruenke's back. Thiessen threw her gloves onto her desk and said: "Adele, you sure got

yourself into a big one now." Thiessen testified later that
Gruenke admitted to beating the old man up. After that,
"she said she got a ride back, that she had an alibi of
someone who was giving her a ride and that's all I know,"
she said. Gruenke told Thiessen she had planned to pick
Barnett up and to kill him because she was so angry with
the old geezer. Their relationship had been friendly at
first but it had become perverted by the old man's
unrelenting lust.

Thiessen tried to counsel her, telling her that forgiveness from God is based on an "inner heart attitude," not
an outside action. She was trying to probe whether
Gruenke was truly remorseful. She asked Gruenke that
if she had to do it again, would she have? The apparent
model of remorse, "she said that if she had known it
would have gone like this and that she would end up getting caught, she wouldn't have done it."

Thiessen asked Gruenke if the killing "looked that
bad." Gruenke admitted she beat Barnett badly. How
badly? "So badly that his guts were hanging out of his
head and there was blood all over."

The pastor wondered aloud how on earth Gruenke
thought she would get away with this. "Adele said she
had it preplanned to be looking like a robbery," Frovich
said. Thiessen remarked that she wasn't a professional
and must have left some traces. Gruenke seemed regret-
ful that she had forgotten to take Barnett's wallet. Had
she done so, his death might have looked like a brutal
robbery.

"She was crying quite a bit at that time. She was

blurting out certain things, one of them was she needed the money to live, for her vitamin therapy, and that he was giving an ultimatum, either you come across or that's it, you are cut off; and she said she was desperate," Frovich said.

"She needed to do something soon because she needed his money to live. She was afraid of dying, if she didn't get her vitamin therapy…She quoted me a scripture, 'the love of money is the root of all evil.'"

The pastor and Frovich decided to call a lawyer and made arrangements for Gruenke to be at his office the next day. "Adele made a comment that she would like to phone Jim Fosty because she felt that he needed to know that she was going to tell everybody the truth because they had made a prearrangement that if she got caught she would not implement [sic] him, so she felt he should know she was going to confess," Frovich said.

That night Gruenke went back to the Frovich residence, where they telephoned Fosty. A half-hour later, a visibly upset Fosty arrived. Gruenke broke the news to him at the kitchen table: she was going to tell the lawyers everything. "He made a comment that this was a stupid plan and he wished he had never gone along with it," Frovich said. Her husband, Bill, stayed in the kitchen talking to Fosty, while Gruenke and Frovich went to a bedroom to talk.

Everything was beginning to unravel. "She felt very guilty about Jim's involvement in it. That she had to get him involved. And she was very upset. She felt like she betrayed him by having to tell the truth but she also wanted him to have the opportunity to say the truth so he could have that feeling of no guilt, and she made a comment that he – that Jim had also hit Phil and she looked a little upset that she had told me that. She said, 'I shouldn't have said that to you,'" Frovich remarked.

Gruenke said Barnett had been killed with a large hammer. Its wooden handle had been burned, destroyed. Barnett, she said, had to be killed no later than Friday, but she didn't explain the reason for such a deadline.

Gruenke had spent the previous week consumed by methods of killing the old man. Drowning him in his bathtub was one way, but she had dismissed it because the pictures of her scattered throughout the apartment would automatically have made her a suspect.

On December 1, Gruenke, Fosty and Janine Frovich waited in the lawyer's office. Fosty said he wished he had known Bill Frovich earlier. "I wish I had known him before the murder. I wouldn't have done it," he told Frovich. At that moment, he asked Frovich if he needed to confess everything he had done. She answered he had to. Just then, the lawyers walked in.

Meanwhile, the police continued to gather evidence. Searching Gruenke's room at her mother's home, they found a will, dated February 22, 1985. It read:

> *"In the event of my death, I, Philip Barnett, being of sound mind and body leave my entire Estate to Miss Adele R. Gruenke presently residing at 214 Stuart Avenue, Winnipeg, Manitoba, R2G 0Y5.*
>
> *I also appoint the said Miss. A.R. Gruenke as Executor of my Estate."*

It is signed by Barnett.

Gruenke was unaware this document had been super-seded by the July 16 will, giving her only interest on the estate.

Two RCMP constables visited James Fosty's house in Birds Hill. They told him they were investigating the homicide of Phil Barnett and warned him he could be charged with being an accessory after the fact. The pair told Fosty they were interested in taking his late-model Grand Am to a garage, apparently to search for more evidence. Fosty was more than accommodating and even offered to drive it there. His reaction got more peculiar all the time.

He invited the officers into the house, even offering to take their coats and asking if they would like something to drink as the television blared in the living room. "He was very hospitable, very co-operative, in fact, very bubbly," one constable recalled.

After Fosty called his counsel, Hersh Wolch, a top Manitoba lawyer, and made arrangements, he went to the washroom and made a nervous joke to the officers. "You better come with me. I have a shot gun." The officers took it lightheartedly but checked the bathroom and left the door ajar, just in case.

In the police car, the officers couldn't shut Fosty up. Not that they wanted to, but he was talking so much that one officer told his colleague to turn on the tape recorder so they wouldn't miss any of it. None of the talk had to do with the arrest, however, as Fosty chatted about skiing, motorcycling and the officers' jobs with the RCMP.

Upon arriving at RCMP headquarters and speaking

with his lawyer, Fosty exercised his right not to speak.
Adele Gruenke, in the meantime, had been picked up
and the pair were jointly charged with first-degree murder. Police believed James Fosty helped Adele Gruenke
kill Phil Barnett near the Chechvala farmhouse between
5 and 6 p.m. on November 28, 1986. Then they drove his
dead body to the highway where it was discovered.

Gruenke and Fosty were placed in the remand centre,
a jail located in Winnipeg's Public Safety Building,
known for its urine-laced floors and lack of mattresses.
On December 4, Adele provided police with a hair
sample. A week later, she gave officers a blood sample,
even though she was under no obligation to do so. It was
evident early on that Gruenke couldn't cut prison life.
She had been sleeping in the middle of the floor and con-
templating suicide.

In January, Gruenke was released on bail and went to
visit Janine Frovich. "She wanted God to get her off. She
felt that if she told the truth that God would all of a sudden – presto – a miracle would happen; she wouldn't have
to go to jail," Frovich recalled. "I said: 'God can't go
against the laws of our government,' that if you commit a
crime by breaking the law you have the consequences of
going to jail if you do wrong." Besides a miraculous
intervention, Gruenke was also looking for Frovich not
to testify at her trial. "I told her I would not lie for her.
She asked me if I would not testify and I said: 'Adele I
cannot do that.' She said: 'You told me you were going to
stick by me' and I said, 'Yes, I will, but I will not lie for
you. I cannot do that.'"

The trial began on October 13, 1987 with jury selection. The Court of Queen's Bench jury was comprised of 12 panel members; seven men, five women. Hersh Wolch was acting for Fosty, while Darcy McCaffrey, another bright light in the legal community, represented Gruenke. Senior Crown Attorney George Dangerfield handled the prosecution, with Madame Justice Ruth Krindle presiding.

Dangerfield presented the prosecution's case with flair and drama. The lanky, grey-haired senior Crown attorney with the authoritarian manner is known for prosecuting the most serious of criminals, including Dwayne Johnston, who was convicted in 1987 of killing Helen Betty Osborne, a Cree Indian girl, in The Pas, Man. in 1971. (See *Conspiracy of Silence* by Lisa Priest, McClelland & Stewart, 1989).

Dangerfield told the jury how Barnett first went to Gruenke for a troubled hip and "a friendship developed beyond the professional." In the fall of 1985, she opened up her own business at Paolo's Hairstyling, using Barnett's money and Fosty's skills at carpentry. After they moved in together, he pestered her for sex. "At this stage, the relationship between the two had changed markedly," Dangerfield said. "That sort of (interest in sexual) activity in a man that age is not unremarkable although some of you may find it unusual. In any event it was not something that Gruenke wished to indulge."

"The prosecution's case is simply this, that Gruenke tiring of these protestations that Barnett was making an insistence that he have sex with her elicited the help of

Fosty and together went to Lorette (Manitoba) with Barnett, together they killed him, together they took his
body to where it was found some 13 km away from where
he was killed and together they made up the story to
cover up what they had done that particular night."

Following Dangerfield's presentation, several police
officers took the stand, describing what they found when
they arrived at the scene and the litany of procedures that
followed.

Maurice Edwin Wolff, a blood expert, testified that he
was brought into the case in early December, after being
told that there were blood stains and splatters in the car,
similar to those found when a victim has been killed by a
gunshot blast. His very precise science involves studying
the patterns and splatters of blood, which can tell him a
great deal about how the victim was slain, what weapon
may have been used and what force was required. Blood,
in this instance, was everywhere – on the dashboard, the
steering wheel, hinges of the car doors and the glove
compartment.

Curved patterns of blood on the Tempo's console
indicated that Philip Barnett had been struck on the back
of the head. "A blow to the back of the head, even a grasp-
ing of the body, head area or shoulder area, and literally
pulling it forward and striking the dash it would do the
same thing," Wolff testified. "The major damage was
done outside."

Similar blood splattering patterns were found in the
left rear wheel well and on the driver's side of James
Fosty's car. Indeed, because most of the blood stains on
Barnett's clothing were found above knee level, in the

torso area, he said it was likely Barnett had been beaten to death while kneeling.

Another expert found blood consistent with Barnett's on a wheel cover seized from Fosty's car. Barnett's blood was also found on the car fabric and in the Grand Am trunk and on the shaft of the nailpuller sold to Bolin.

RCMP Corp. Doug Agnew of the commercial crime section prepared a net worth statement of Barnett determining that he was worth $248,408, excluding the value of his furniture. He also discovered that Barnett had written cheques to Gruenke totalling $26,342.64, not including a credit card he arranged for her and any purchases she made on it. Also bought for her was a diamond pendant, jewelry, ladies' boots, purse, hosiery, gloves, ski equipment, a gold chain and a $600 leather dress. Barnett sold their house for $93,500.

Adele Gruenke's former boyfriend, Garth Davisson, testified that Gruenke had telephoned him on November 29 to say that Barnett had been murdered.

"She wanted to know where I was Friday night and she told [me] that the cops would be coming to interview me and she told that he [Barnett] picked up a hitchiker and was murdered and that was it."

Testifying in her own defence, Gruenke recalled how she had met Barnett. He pressured her for sexual favours and she eventually couldn't take it anymore. At times, he became so angry about Gruenke's unwillingness to "come across" that he threatened to hurt her mother should she ever move out of the house. Matters came to a head on November 28, when Gruenke arranged to meet Barnett that evening.

She asked Fosty to follow her and be a "guardian angel," she testified. She instructed Fosty to sit in a car down the street while she talked to Barnett. That's when Barnett began to drive, and Fosty followed them. During the drive, she asked Barnett why he was so insistent about making her do things she clearly didn't want to do. "Then he got right in about, you know, the two years that he had wasted, all of this money he had put into me and he figured by spending all of this money that I would be grateful to him. That it wouldn't be that hard to convince me that I was doing him a big favour by engaging in sexual practices with him."

Barnett took her through a "big guilt trip" about how she was a failure in life. "When it got to the point that I didn't want to be around him any more, I told him that he could stop the car because I wasn't going to stand for this any more."

Barnett made fun of her. "He had me all the way out there [near Lorette] and no one was going to be there to rescue me and that I would have a hell of a long way to walk home. In my hysterics, I told him that Jim Fosty knew everything that was going on and that he was following in his car behind."

Angered, Barnett said he wouldn't stop the car. Gruenke threatened to jump out if he didn't. "So I opened my door and he grabbed onto me and I thought of this perverted old man touching me, just made me so sick that I just wanted to get out of that car so badly." Barnett slowed the car down, but didn't let go of Gruenke "so I picked up this wooden handle that was on the floor in the passenger seat. I picked it up and I started to hit him and the door was open and finally he let go and I fell out of the car."

Barnett got out of the car and ran to the passenger side. Gruenke stumbled to her feet and began to run down the highway, searching in the dark and the cold for Fosty. But Barnett grabbed onto her and tried to stuff her back into the car. "I can't remember and, I was wrestling with him, and I just remember being on the ground and him, he was hammering on my chest and the next thing I remember is Jim's feet come running up."

After that, there were "a lot of black spots" and holes in Gruenke's memory. "The next thing I knew Phil was laying beside me all covered in blood." Then she noticed Barnett bleeding in the passenger's side and became hysterical.

Fosty told her to get a grip on herself. He told her to get into Barnett's car and follow him in his. She jumped into the Tempo and began to drive, thinking they were going to the hospital or for help. "I don't remember driving the car. I don't remember going into the ditch. I don't even remember being in Fosty's car."

After that, they went to the car wash and Fosty kept telling her to get a grip on herself. There wasn't anything they could do, he said. She knew nothing of the nail-puller, she said, and, in fact, she hadn't seen it until the preliminary hearing. They went and changed, then went to the Nor-Villa and she felt "pretty shaky, pretty confused. The whole thing didn't seem like reality."

After that, they went for a pizza. "At that time we decided that if and when the police would come and question me or both of us that we would say that – what we were doing the night before, which was, we had gone to Kildonan Place." They also made a pact: if one of them took the blame, they wouldn't implicate the other.

Two days later, when Gruenke met with Thiessen and Frovich, "I had decided that I was going to take the whole shot myself." Distraught, depressed, Gruenke told the court she had wanted to kill herself.

Under cross-examination by Hersh Wolch, Gruenke said Fosty had a lot of friends and not an enemy in the world. A man with a smile on his face all the time, Fosty was never angry. He was a down-to-earth, no-frills kind of guy. And, more importantly, she told court, she never saw Fosty strike a blow at Barnett. With that, Wolch had all that he needed. He had elicited that Fosty was a nice farm boy who hadn't hurt Barnett. There was nothing to do now except sit down.

It was Dangerfield who had to poke holes in Gruenke's obviously shallow explanation of what had occurred. He suggested she had fabricated the story about her dying from leukemia because she wanted to keep Barnett's money rolling in. Gruenke said she didn't know why she accepted large sums of money from Barnett, she just did. She never planned to kill Phil Barnett.

"But you never had leukemia?" Dangerfield asked.

"I suppose I didn't," Gruenke responded.

"And you knew it."

"No," she replied. "I had all the symptoms my dad had before they found out he had leukemia and he suffered for four years or five years and they never bothered to investigate really what was wrong with him."

"But you told (Garth) Davisson that was a lie."

" I never told Davisson it was a lie. I told him that I didn't know for sure what was wrong with me."

Dangerfield wasn't having any of it. "You lied all throughout, didn't you? To the police. To Ms. Frovich. To Thiessen. Mmm mmm?"

"It didn't seem...."

"It's a lie, isn't it, that you were frightened of Barnett, afraid of his sexual advances? The truth of the matter is that you wanted his money. You cannot explain all of the indignities you put up with unless you agree with me that what you really wanted from Barnett is his money."

"That's not true."

"And to ensure that you would, you and Fosty beat him to death in that roadway in Lorette, you still had his will, didn't you?"

"No I didn't."

Dr. Fred Shane, a psychiatrist who is frequently called to testify in criminal cases, saw Gruenke six times and evaluated her for the defence. He conducted hypnosis on her and injected her with sodium amytal, commonly known as truth serum. In his opinion, "she certainly appeared ostensibly genuine and credible." After meeting with her and exploring her background, he thought it unlikely that she could have planned something of this magnitude.

Some parts of her relationship with Barnett were affectionate. "She was hoping to recapture some warmth through an older man, which she never had from her father, and I think this was a precipitating factor, but, at the same time, I think the relationship was bad for her in a sense because she moved in with a father-like figure and accentuated those symptoms."

He said she was guilt-ridden about Fosty and was blocking certain events of the murder from her memory. Under cross-examination, Shane said she was caught in a "very dependent, very hostile ambivalent relationship" with Barnett. He didn't think that it was at all related to money.

Dangerfield, known for his sardonic manner, commented to Shane: "May I say you sound remarkably like her?" The comment touched off some verbal combat. Shane said he resented that comment, that he was not a lie-detector test. "She is under a lot of pressure and she had fantasies of harming the old man and she talked about it openly. She didn't try to hide that from me. She's very open about that."

Describing Gruenke as a decent, good girl, McCaffrey said his client was pursuing her own career as best she could in the face of being very gullible and vulnerable. Barnett created a dependency and lured Gruenke into the relationship, all the while filling his head with sexual fantasies.

In a later interview, McCaffrey said Gruenke wasn't the most intelligent person around and "this old boy was bent on carnal pleasure." Gruenke was a "pretty open person. She wasn't a sophisticated Mata Hari. I think the old boy was gradually putting himself into a position of power."

The troublesome part of the case, McCaffrey said, was Gruenke's conversations with the pastor and church counsellor. It was his view that she made incriminating statements to them to cover for Fosty. In arguing her innocence, McCaffrey conceded his client may well be guilty of accessory after the fact, but that was not the issue. "I am asking you to release her from the nightmare and send her home to her mother."

Wolch took the podium next. He said there was no motive for Fosty to kill Barnett. He didn't know about Barnett's will and there was no evidence that he was anything more than a friend to Adele Gruenke. Describing Fosty as a hard-working country boy, Wolch said he believed his client was convinced that Gruenke was dying, that he felt sorry for her, and that she was being unreasonably pressured to have sexual relations with an older man.

He said Fosty saw Gruenke being attacked by a man who wanted perverted sex from her. If the jury found that Fosty did strike a blow, Wolch asked them to consider for what reason. "The reason being that he will be rescuing a girl who he cared for, for good reason, and was frightened." Either he is not guilty, or he is guilty of manslaughter, Wolch said.

Madame Justice Ruth Krindle charged the jury, saying they could find the pair guilty of first or second-degree murder or manslaughter, or not guilty. On October 23, 1987, 10 days after the trial commenced, the jury found both guilty of first-degree murder. The sentence carries an automatic penalty of 25 years imprisonment before parole eligibility. Both are serving time in Kingston.

Adele Gruenke subsequently appealed her conviction

claiming that her admissions to the pastor and counsellor
for the Victorious Faith Centre Church should not have
been allowed as evidence at her trial. But Chief Justice
Antonio Lamer, writing in November 1991 for the
Supreme Court of Canada, concluded that religious confessions are not automatically privileged. Unlike a con-
ference with a lawyer, a conversation with a pastor is not
"inextricably linked with the justice system" but he did
acknowledge that a religious confession could be privileged in some circumstances.

The hardest part, her brother says, is waiting for the
day she is released, if ever. "We talk to her and she's still
struggling," Rudy said. "Some of those people in prison
have no value in their life at all. You don't trust anybody
in there. I know she doesn't."

THREE

A Confusion of Gender

THE doctor looked up from his file and into the expectant eyes of Robert Pearson.

The diagnosis was grim: Lung cancer.

If Robert Pearson felt frightened at all, he didn't show it. Not to his twin stepsons who had driven him to the hospital that fall day in 1972. Not to the doctor. Temperamentally Robert Pearson wasn't one to fret. As bad as lung cancer may be, he wasn't going to let it get him down.

The doctor tried to accentuate the positive. Diagnosis had been early. There were just a few spots on the lungs of the 55-year-old Toronto cab driver. Moreover, modern medicine was constantly finding new and better treatments for cancer, he said. With radiation therapy, the cabbie could get better.

Pearson wanted that medical miracle. His life was good and he wanted it to stay that way. He had a loving wife, Irene, whom he adored, twin step-sons Dennis and

Donald who had never hesitated to call him "Pop," and a job he seemed made for.

When Pearson first experienced chest pains that year, his family thought it might be his heart. When he returned to their Parkdale home in westend Toronto with the news about the cancer, Irene Pearson couldn't help but be terrified. She didn't want to lose this man who had given her so much happiness.

Almost every case of lung cancer is caused by cigarette smoking and Pearson's was no different. He liked to puff on them during the dead time of driving a taxicab or on breaks in the coffee shops while chatting to his friends. Waiting for a fare, he would occassionally light one up just for something to do. However, when he heard the word cancer, he dropped cigarettes cold turkey. He also took a similar approach to his treatment. "He said: 'I'll just go down and get rid of that,'" Irene would recall later. Every day for several weeks, Pearson went down to Princess Margaret Hospital for radiation therapy and check-ups.

Perhaps it was this matter-of-fact attitude, combined with a steely determination to live, that paid off. He just didn't believe he would die. Within months, his cancer went into remission. Doctors told him the next five years would be the real test. Often, cancer that goes can return in bigger, more horrifying proportions. There's just no telling who gets the breaks in life. By 1977 Robert Pearson had passed the five-year mark and was deemed to be "cured" of the often-fatal disease. If this wasn't a miracle, the family thought, they didn't know what was. Irene Pearson now slept soundly.

Oddly, after being given this clean bill of health, Pearson began to light up the occasional Rothman's cigarette. Perhaps he was a bit of a fatalist, or he felt if he could beat cancer, he could beat anything. Whatever the reason, he was not averse to puffing the odd cigarette while waiting for a fare, still a drastic cut from his former one-pack-a-day habit. Besides, smoking was one of those things that went along with being a cabbie. And Pearson loved driving hack. He loved the drive, the feel of the wheel in his grip. He loved being his own boss, meeting people, and giving advice. The short grey-haired man with a puckered face and prominent laugh lines could listen sympathetically to passengers at length and comfort others without pointing a finger. He was also a veritable fount of trivia and small talk. Horse-race results, sports scores, weather reports – he knew them all like he knew the Toronto streets he'd first explored as a youth.

Despite his small stature, Pearson was a sturdy man with muscular arms. This may have been the result of all the loading and unloading he did. Groceries, furniture, you name it, Pearson moved it for friends, fares, or anyone else who requested his help. Ask the man a favour, he wouldn't say no. He *couldn't* say no. He was just that kind of guy.

Irene Pearson felt she had lucked out marrying such a man. Compared to her first husband, Pearson was a gem, steadfast in his devotion to her.

In the spring of 1943, after Dennis and Donald had been born, Irene's first husband was overseas, serving as a corporal in the Canadian Army. The couple exchanged letters and he sent her parcels from England, where he was stationed. Her husband returned in 1944 or 1945 – Irene can't remember which – and by that time they were like total strangers. It was obvious from the first day he arrived home, this marriage wasn't going to work. "We didn't know each other anymore so we decided to drop it." From that point, Irene saw little of her former spouse nor did he take much interest in his sons.

Robert Pearson was like a godsend. Irene had known him all her life and they had been friends in their working-class neighborhood. At the time their friendship sparked into something more, he was living with a male friend on Dufferin Street in Toronto's west end. He liked her spirit, her sense of humour, her strength, her blonde hair. She loved his eyes, his easy manner, his magnanimous nature. In 1948, he moved into her house on Pearson Ave.

Loving Irene meant loving her sons and he treated them like his own, maybe even better than his own children. Being a father wasn't new to Robert Pearson. He had two sons and a daughter from a previous marriage. That marriage had floundered in part because his wife didn't like the hours her cabbie husband kept. Asking Pearson to change his job was like asking him to peel off his own skin.

Irene knew and accepted what hours a cabbie kept – she had two brothers and two brother-in-laws who were taxidrivers. She didn't try to change anyone or anything. Besides, the time he spent away didn't matter to her because when he wasn't at work, he was with her.

Like Pearson, she had learned an art very few do in

life: to enjoy what she had instead of complaining bitterly about what she didn't have. She expected little, demanded nothing, and got everything in return. It was an existence as beautiful as it was ordinary.

The day she married Pearson – June 18, 1951 – was "the happiest day in my life." She was 29 at the time and her sons were eight.

Although it was tough getting by on a cabbie's income, the times were good, and the laughs were many. Every Wednesday – Pearson's day off – they would go to a friend's home, sometimes to play cards, other times to chat. Occassionally, they would go for vacations to Irene's sister's cottages in Minden and Oakridge. It didn't matter where they went, as long as they were together.

Even her sons seemed to love Pearson more than their own biological father. "One time the boys asked me if I would be upset if they looked up their natural father," Irene recalled. "I said I wouldn't be but they never looked him up. Bob was their father."

This kind of love was the glue that kept the family together, especially when they had some tough blows. Irene's older sister, Ruth, died on her birthday – October 13, 1977 – from cancer of the neck and throat. It was a terrible time. Ruth's husband had died the winter before and Irene had spent the past six or seven months caring for her dying sister.

At one time Parkdale, the Pearsons' neighbourhood, had been a place where Toronto's well-off lived. Just far enough away from the bustle of downtown and the squalor of Cabbagetown, it offered virtually immediate proximity to the beaches of Lake Ontario. As the city grew, the more affluent moved further west, to such areas as High Park and Baby Point. More and more of the working-class and unemployed began moving into Parkdale's huge homes with their intricate woodwork and spacious interiors. Many of the homes, Victorian, Edwardian and Art Deco in style, suffered from neglect while others were renovated and subdivided into duplexes, rental units, and rooming houses. By the seventies, the area had a reputation as being a place for derelicts, drugs abusers, petty criminals, and struggling immigrants.

Sunday, April 9, 1978 seemed like it was going to be another ordinary day for the Pearsons. After the alarm sounded, Robert Pearson, 61, got out of bed, showered, shaved, put on his clothes, then, after kissing his wife goodbye at 6:30 a.m., headed for work.

Later that day, Irene felt uneasy. A man of routine, Robert Pearson always called his wife between 3 and 4 p.m. to see if she needed anything from the store. This was the first day in 30 years he hadn't called. Irene started to fret but figured her husband had probably got tied up on a call, or something. "I was sitting at the front door when the doorbell rang and two policemen were there," Irene recalled. The officers told her that her husband's cab had been found blocking a rooming-house driveway on Springhurst Avenue, just eight blocks from home. "I said: 'That's not my Bob. He wouldn't park across a driveway.'"

The officers explained that they and the building owner had made enquiries in the three-storey rooming house at 142 Springhurst, looking for Pearson but couldn't find him. Pearson's taxi company also hadn't heard from him in several hours. Meanwhile, his car's meter was still running. "Right there, I knew something was wrong," she said.

A frantic Irene called her sons and brothers to tell them what had happened and they soon joined the ranks of the worried and fearful. Police had Sunnyside Taxi #1446 impounded and notified the cab's owner, George Keetch, Pearson's brother-in-law. Something clearly had gone awry, but what?

Constables Mark Tully and David Sproule canvassed the building at 142 Springhurst and were told by several tenants that loud, banging noises had come from room #7, located on the first floor. Sandra Lee Gauthier said she had seen the taxi stop in front of the driveway at about 11 a.m. and two men approach the front door of the rooming house. A short while later, she heard noises coming from apartment #7, noises that lasted about ten minutes.

Two other tenants, Donald Lawrence Levesque, and Patrick John Neilan also heard noises from #7. Neilan heard a man yelp: "Help me! Help me!" He thought it was a domestic argument and left it at that.

When they heard the tenants speak of a man's piercing screams, that was enough for officers to ask the owner, David Thorpe, for a key to the room.

When uniformed police officers opened Room #7 at

7:54 p.m., they caught a glimpse of hell: Pearson's, bloodied, lifeless body was stuffed beneath a fold-out chesterfield. The room was a mess. Blood was spread all over the bathroom tiles and the room was flooded with water. Despite an attempted wash-up, Pearson was swaddled in his blood-stained clothing. An autopsy would reveal the cause of death as "stab wounds of the lung," but it wasn't the only wound Robert Pearson suffered....

Thorpe told police he noticed that the tenant of the room, a Susan Lynn Wood, had been cleaning up some spilled water on the stairs between the first and second floors earlier in the day. She blamed the problem on an overflowing shower, the result of dumping "kitty litter" down the drain. A search for Wood in the house drew a blank. Clearly she was the strongest suspect. But what about that man Pearson had been seen with?

Sergeant Julian Fantino of Metro Toronto's homicide division got the call to go to the rooming house at about 8:30 p.m. Arriving with his partner, Staff Sergeant Walter Tyrrell, he was stunned by the carnage. "I couldn't believe what I was seeing," Fantino said in a recent interview. "I thought it was a very, very bad dream and sooner or later I would wake up from it."

An hour after Fantino and Tyrrell arrived at the rooming house, the telephone rang in Wood's suite. Fantino picked it up. There was dead silence. He hung up. Then it rang a second time. After a few seconds pause a young girl's voice broke in: "Do you know who I am?"

Fantino guessed it was probably Susan Lynn Wood.

He tried to engage her in conversation to keep her talking, to try to convince her to meet with police.

Wood agreed to talk to Fantino but she said she was concerned about what would happen to her. He told her they would have to talk it out: they should meet and get everything straightened out once and for all. The caller seemed interested but cagey. Fantino adopted a reassuring tone, telling the caller it was best that they meet.

After about five minutes of negotiations, Fantino managed to persuade her to meet him and his partner. Wood suggested a church at the northeast corner of Dufferin Street and Eglinton Avenue. When the pair of police officers pulled up to the corner they saw a short, slender, young girl. She was standing on the corner looking rather tomboyish. The girl with wavy, shoulder-length brown hair, a turned-up nose and pretty eyes, climbed into the back of the police car and gave her name, address, telephone number, and her place of employment. Her name was Susan Lynn Wood and she was 16. And, yes, she had killed the cabbie.

As Fantino and his partner were talking to Wood in their cruiser, Irene Pearson was at home trying to cope with the dreadful news. Officers had returned to her home a second time that day to say her husband had been found dead.

They couldn't, however, bring themselves to tell Pearson that her husband had been castrated. They were torn with telling her the man she had depended on, day or night, to be consistently loving and kind, had vanished from her life. Did she really need to know how? "I hoped he didn't have to suffer," she said. "I couldn't live with myself if I thought he did."

Wood, in the meantime, was taken into police custody and formally charged with first-degree murder. She was the youngest female to ever be charged with murder in Metro. After she was cautioned, she gave police a statement that was later read out in court.

Wood said she had hailed a cab at King Street and Jameson Avenue in Parkdale between 10:30 and 11 a.m. on April 9 and asked the driver to help her move some furniture from Springhurst Avenue to her mother's place. The driver was Robert Pearson. Ever amenable, he agreed to help her.

Entering Wood's room, he was directed to pick up the television set. As he did so, Wood took a baseball bat and brought it down on his head once, twice, several times. "Help me! Help me!" he cried, but no one came to the old man's assistance.

Pearson slumped to the floor whereupon Wood said she attacked him with a kitchen knife, stabbing him twice, then pulling his body into the shower. She left it running to rinse off the blood.

"I kept on hitting him and hitting him. Then I stabbed him. He took such a long time to die," Wood said later at her trial.

After Pearson took his last breath, Wood said: "I cleaned him up a bit, then I cut off his penis, then I took his jacket and sweater off, then I put it in a green garbage bag, then I took the money out of his pockets and his keys, then I put him under the bed, then I covered him with a sleeping bag and some pillows, then I left."

Wood went straight to her girlfriend's apartment, #202 at 80 Grandravine Drive, located in Downsview, northwest of where the crime occurred. Wood and her girlfriend, Sandra Marshall, had been "going together" for one year. Marshall and she had engaged in the odd "make-out" session, which included heavy petting, yet somehow Marshall hadn't figured out that her *boyfriend* was, in fact, her *girlfriend*. Wood looked, walked and talked like a boy. To her co-workers and most acquaintances, she wasn't Susan Lynn Wood but Adam Thomas Hazel.

Had Wood not got involved in a fight with a boy at a McDonald's Restaurant in Downsview two nights before, she might have kept her gender a secret. The police had to break up the brawl that April 7. When Wood/Hazel was pulled into the station, officers soon discovered this "boy" was a girl, her breasts bound flat with pieces of cardboard. Since Sandra Marshall accompanied Wood/Hazel to the police station, officers notified her father of her whereabouts — and the strange nature of Sandra's "boyfriend."

When Sandra Marshall questioned Wood/Hazel about her gender, "he" denied being a she. But Sandra's father, Brian Marshall, was having none of it. He wanted proof that Adam Hazel was, in fact, a *he*.

Realizing that her double life was on the verge of being exposed, Susan Lynn Wood tried to find a way out. In desperation, she hit upon what she thought was the only solution. "I'll kill a cabdriver, slice off his genitals, then glue them to myself."

On April 9, she hailed a taxi in Parkdale and lured the

cabbie up to her room. After carving off his penis and testicles, she affixed the sexual organs to herself. "I used Krazee Glue. It sticks to anything." Once the genitals were glued tight to her labia, she went to the Marshall residence and unzipped her pants before Sandra's father.

Finally, she thought, he would let well enough alone. Mr. Marshall, however, looked at the genitals with a skeptical eye. In the apartment sauna, Adam "dropped his pants and I could see what appeared to be a penis and testicles," he said. "But the colour didn't appear real. It looked pale, like synthetic rubber."

"I said, 'I'm sorry, Adam, that isn't real. You're a girl.' I could see what looked like Scotch tape, I reached down and lifted the testicles up and I could see her female organs," he testified in court later. This double-life came as a surprise to the elder Marshall, who had frequently boxed with what he thought was his daughter's boyfriend. "He walked and talked and certainly acted like a boy....I was totally fooled by this situation," Marshall testified.

Later, Wood told her girlfriend that "your father has got it drummed into his head that I'm a girl and he won't even give me a chance," Sandra Marshall testified. When "Adam" showed Sandra the penis, "it appeared to be glued on. I told her I didn't think it was real. I knew then she was a girl. I thought she needed help." Later, while in custody, Wood gave police pubic and scalp hair samples and led them to a high-rise apartment building near her girlfriend's apartment, where she had dumped the two tubes of glue she had used to paste the genitals onto herself.

And where were the missing genitals? Wood led officers back to the church at Eglinton and Dufferin, where
she pointed to a clump of bright, purple lilies. Stashed in
the earth was a brown paper bag. In it, were Mr. Pearson's
private parts. Doctors had determined that Robert Pearson had been dead before being castrated.

It was quite an amazing story. A grotesque story. And
"you could tell she was a very mixed-up, confused,
young lady," Fantino recalled. "As far as I was concerned, she was very distressed."

Fantino is a hard-nosed cop who is now chief of London, Ontario's police force. Such sympathetic words
don't slip easily from his lips. After all, Susan Wood did
kill a man. But this case bothered him more than he
thought. "I'm normally very good at distancing myself
because I have no agenda other than getting the facts and
presenting those facts. But I found this case to be a real
test," he said. "Tyrrell and I would look at one another
and all of a sudden, we would be independently wondering if this was real....You could probably never get
another replay [of this set of variables]. Even as I talk
about it, I still can't believe that I was involved in this."

A hard-working Italian Catholic with a love of family
life, Fantino feels nothing is more sacred than the unit of
wife, husband, and children. It is the security net, the
thing you draw your strength from. Yet clearly Susan
Lynn Wood didn't seem to have much of that.

Wood didn't seem to have much of anything, for that
matter. A shabbily-furnished room, a job at a gas station
and no friends except for Sandra Marshall. And how she
craved her affection. It was her only close relationship,

the only thing that gave her life meaning. Without that, she had nothing. Born September 5, 1961 in Westmoreland County, New Brunswick, Wood had lived a deprived life after her parents split up. Coming from a background riddled with poverty and mental illness, according to psychiatrists who testified at her trial later, Wood faced a bleak future.

The sex in this killing, Fantino said, was a matter of convenience. "This particular person – given her limited ability to rationalize – was faced with this incredible need to face this situation [of being found out she was a girl]," Fantino said.

Irene Pearson didn't know her husband had been castrated until several days after his death. Her family, not wanting to exacerbate her grief, decided to withhold that information. Toronto newspapers would land on her coffee table with stories about her husband, lines of which were blacked out with a magic marker, courtesy of her sister. However, one day she was listening to the radio when the news came on. There was an item about a demonstration that taxi drivers had planned in reaction to Pearson's death. The announcer described how Pearson had been castrated and, upon hearing this, an aghast Irene ran downstairs to her sister's home on the first floor and asked if it was true. "It was a terrible way for him to go. He was too good a man," Irene said. "I just thought he was hit and died instantly."

Four days after his death, Irene kissed her husband one last goodbye minutes before the closed-casket funeral began at Park Lawn Cemetery in Toronto.

"What can you say other than I miss you and I'm so sorry," she asked, still obviously struck with grief.

About 100 mourners, including 50 taxi drivers, paid their respects. At the funeral, a petition calling for the reinstatement of capital punishment was circulated among angry taxidrivers. Later, they carried it in their cars, asking passengers to back up their cause.

Their petition got an added boost on July 24 when an Ontario Supreme Court judge agreed to release Pearson's killer on $8,300 bail. Within moments of hearing that news, cabdrivers were planning a protest. On July 27 a convoy of 60 taxis, preceded by a yellow pick-up truck, drove up University Avenue toward the Ontario legislature at Queen's Park. They honked their horns and turned on their lights before blocking the driveway in front of the legislature, as ten Metro police officers and Ontario government security guards watched the drivers from behind the blockades.

"They had loud speakers in the streets and lines and lines of cabs," Irene recalled. "It really put the fear into me when I heard she got bail." During that time, Irene was prone to panic attacks. "If my grandson was late five minutes, I'd be out on the street looking for him. It was terrifying when she was on bail."

The cabbies' protest had an immediate effect: Ontario Attorney-General Roy McMurtry came onto the steps of the legislature to promise he would review the transcript of the bail order and make a decision on it within 24 hours. "I am very concerned at this particular order," McMurtry told reporters and drivers. "We may very well apply to the chief justice of Ontario for leave to have the bail order reviewed." Although he acknowledged he hadn't seen the transcript, he said he was "rather surprised" bail had been granted.

The following day, McMurtry ordered an appeal against the bail order after lengthy discussions with senior ministry officials. Crown law officers were to ask Ontario's chief justice to send the bail decision to the Court of Appeal. On August 3, Associate Chief Justice Bert Mackinnon listened to the review application for two hours and determined that the case was of sufficient importance to be sent to the higher court. He imposed a publication ban on the proceedings. On August 10, three justices of the Ontario Supreme Court of Appeal ordered Wood's bail revoked. Chief Justice William Howland with Mr. Justices Charles Dubbin and G. Arthur Martin put a publication ban on the proceedings and, simply stated, the release order was set aside. Wood was returned to jail where she stayed until her trial began in Toronto on December 15, 1978.

It was later discovered that one night before Pearson was slain, Wood had stabbed a 15-year-old boy, apparently with the intention of slicing off his genitals. The boy, however, managed to escape her clutches, albeit with a collapsed lung, and was later treated in hospital. She was subsequently charged with attempted murder.

At the trial for the Pearson murder a seventeen-year-old Wood, represented by lawyer Hugh Silverman, entered a plea of not guilty by reason of insanity before a jury and Chief Justice Gregory Evans. Silverman admitted the facts of the case but said he would attempt to prove that she was insane at the time of the offence. To be ruled insane, a jury must find that she was unable to appreciate the nature and quality of the act.

Irene Pearson didn't go to court because "my relatives wouldn't let me go. They told me it would be better if I didn't."

Testifying in her defence, psychiatrist Dr. Peter Rowsell said Wood had an "absolute, imperative need to get a penis," attach it to herself and prove she was a boy. If she was unable to acquire one, she saw it as the end to her year-long relationship with Sandra Marshall. He termed her behaviour as "sick with a capital 'S'. I think it's grotesque, a monstrous act." Years later, Rowsell would observe that the chief person Susan Wood was trying to deceive was herself. "That was the utter pathos of the whole thing. On one level she knew that it didn't make sense but on another level it was imperative she kill someone to get it [penis]. It was pure craziness."

Rowsell said that Wood was, in fact, insane at the time she committed the murder. Neglected as a child, she had been confused about her sexual identity and preferred to play with boys in her early years. At age 12, she was compressing her breasts with cardboard because "she hated them very intensely and had thoughts of cutting them off."

A deadly combination of hopelessness, helplessness and worthlessness led her to commit the crime. "She was hardly planning for the long term. It was an immediate need. She thought she would feel close to somebody

[Sandra Marshall], if only for a few hours. Getting a penis was a way of staving off total abandonment while holding onto a human being she loved and affirming her belief that 'she should be a man.'"

Clinical psychologist Alan Long testified that Wood's real world in terms of emotional satisfaction revolved around her being Adam Hazel. She became panicky when that world was threatened. "Clearly, she was a schizoid personality," Long said later. A schizoid person, according to Long, is one who is very shy and introverted, who lives in a fantasy world. "Often their background is one of emotional deprivation. They are weak-looking people. They are vulnerable people and they can become psychotic."

Wood didn't need drugs or alcohol to commit this bizarre act, he said. It was loneliness that was the driving force. "If you take loneliness as the basic problem, it's a crushing kind of experience and people will take unusual steps to cope with it." Describing Wood as cooperative and bright, Long said she told her story with consistency. "The tough part was making the decision on how much she was responsible for what she did from a legal point of view. Unless the person is blatantly delusional, you have to examine all possibilities – you're always looking for inconsistencies [in her story]."

To agree she was psychotic at the time, Long noted, he had to believe that Wood felt her world was coming to an end and a quick solution was the only remedy. "People like this experience a terrible anxiety. It's impossible to explain the inner hell they're going through." In all his years of examining murderers and psychotics, Long to this day vividly remembers the case of Susan Lynn Wood. "It was very unusual. I must say it [the murder and castration] was a unique solution to a problem."

Another psychiatrist, Pieter Butler, testified that Wood could require treatment for many years. "At the moment she's an unsafe person," he said. Another doctor said that at some future date, Wood could be a candidate for a sex-change operation.

Testimony ended after three days and the jury of eight women and four men deliberated for a little more than three hours before finding Susan Lynn Wood, also known as Adam Thomas Hazel, not guilty of the charge of first-degree murder by reason of insanity.

Garbed in a man's winter jacket, blue jeans, a sports shirt and construction boots, Wood remained expressionless as the verdict was given. Moments after this jury was discharged, Evans also found her not guilty by reason of insanity on the charge of attempted murder arising from the failed castration of a 15-year-old boy the day before the Pearson murder.

Wood was ordered confined indefinitely to the psychiatric hospital at St. Thomas, located near London, Ont., pending annual reviews of her case.

One person who was not happy with the verdict was Irene Pearson. "How can they rule her insane when she tried it to two men two days in a row?" she still asks angrily. For her, "there isn't a day that goes by where I don't think about Bob." She still can't walk down Springhurst Avenue and not see the big, tall house where he died without crying.

Sadly, Wood's incarceration didn't end Irene's

problems and pain. Left with no life insurance and a 15-year-old grandson to support, she had to live on a monthly family benefit of $297 while facing expenditures of $400 a month.

A year after her husband's death, Irene Pearson went to the Metro Licensing Commission to try and obtain a cabbie's licence – one her husband had been offered two months before his death but declined to take because of he didn't feel in the best of health. Then-student lawyer John Nunziata of Parkdale Community Legal Services, who went on to become a Liberal MP and Solicitor General critic, told the commission that had Pearson taken out the licence, it would have been passed on to Irene, providing her with a $500-a-month income.

In the late seventies, a new cab licence, which was given out in small numbers, cost, officially, $5,000, exclusive of car and equipment. But because of their scarcity, these same licences often went for $35,000 each. In her submission, Irene said: "I just want a licence so that I can rent it out, and get an income from it. It's not that I plan to sell it, or anything. The commission can even put a stipulation on the licence and say I can't sell it," she told *The Toronto Star*.

If her request was granted, cabbies offered to raise the $5,000 for the licence. "I don't want to look as if I'm trying to cash in on my husband's death," she was reported as saying. "I have got to live, and I have to look after Robbie. But I also don't want to sponge off the taxpayers and take money from them. I would much rather have this licence to give me an income."

She was turned down twice. Then in May 1979 the Criminal Injuries Compensation Board awarded her $500 a month for life, plus $1,000 to cover her husband's funeral expenses and $5,000 for the loss of spousal income.

In 1980, just as Irene began to feel the pain subside and her life could start anew, she discovered that police had given a slide presentation at a Toronto church, which featured pictures of her mutilated husband. The Sunday presentation, which occurred just before Christmas, was conducted by a city police staff sergeant at the request of a pastor. It depicted victims of some of the city's most notorious murders. After the ghoulish slide slow, the pastor delivered a sermon favouring capital punishment.

An extremely distraught Irene made her displeasure known and Metro police agreed to destroy the slides of her husband if she promised not to sue. She agreed.

Today, Irene Pearson continues to live in Parkdale and proudly displays her large wedding portrait of her and Robert. She plays cards with her girlfriends and, after three tries, she finally obtained her driver's licence.

Wood, meanwhile, spent several years in therapy in St. Thomas before a panel determined she was well enough to be let out. There is no way to find out precisely when she was released. But one thing is certain: she did change her name and enter society again, this time as a woman.

FOUR

Springflower

WILLIAM Linklater had asked her the same question, off and on, for seven years. He was determined to ask Khristine Snowshoe to marry him for seven more until she said yes. Finally, in the spring of 1976, they were wed. They settled in his home in Old Crow, a tiny settlement near the Arctic Circle.

At 19, Khristine's dreams of a fantasy life with a prince were finally coming true. He built her a log cabin and worked hard at his job as an oil-rigger. At night, they snuggled and dreamed of what their babies would look like. Khristine, part Loucheux Indian and part Inuit, dreamed that they would have a son first, followed by a daughter.

At first, she thrived among the people of Old Crow, a community of 180 persons located 112 km inside the Arctic Circle and 770 km north of Whitehorse in the Yukon. Named after a revered chief, Walking Crow, who died more than a century earlier, many of Old Crow's residents were Loucheux Indians, living in log cabins scattered along the Porcupine River.

The Loucheux had settled at New Rampart House near the Alaska boundary in the 1870s when their original village around Fort Yukon was discovered to be on American soil. When a smallpox epidemic hit in 1911, it wiped out dozens and the survivors moved to the muskrat breeding grounds at the confluence of the Crow and Porcupine rivers.

Although Old Crow had survived some difficult times, it now had a new problem affecting it: alcohol. Plane-loads of booze were all but eroding the Loucheux's ways of life. Parties often lasted for days, ending only when the bottles were empty. Other times, those with a knack for making bootleg liquor made moonshine. Those lucky enough to stumble into the right cabin would get a swig.

People would complain that work in Old Crow got done only when the booze ran out. Along with the booze came alcoholism and a battery of other problems, including wife-beating, thefts and assaults. They were problems often witnessed but rarely talked about in the community.

In the midst of all this, William and Khristine were a couple in love with a lot in common. They both seemed to thrive on the traditional ways of the north and had a passion for skiing that led them to compete in the Arctic Games. At 13, four years after she began to ski, Khristine won a gold medal at the Canadian cross-country ski championships and travelled the continent as a member of Canada's junior cross-country ski team. She seemed destined to participate in the Winter Olympics.

That hope all but vanished at the age of 16 when her role at home became more than she could handle. Born Khristine Mabel Snowshoe on March 22, 1956, she was the second eldest of five daughters; her sisters were Louise, Audrey, Pamela and Effie. As Khristine's father had left when she was a baby, she'd had to carry the load of caring for the younger ones. "I had to come home to my sisters and I quit school and skiing," she said in an interview from Fort McPherson, Northwest Territories.

Born and raised in Fort McPherson, Khristine's mother grew overprotective of her daughter. And with good reason. Should Khristine leave, she would lose her water-fetcher, food-catcher and diaper-changer. Living in a remote area meant more work. Few homes in McPherson had electricity or running water. Residents would lug pails of water from the nearby Porcupine River. Homes were heated by wooden stoves. Dinners consisted of caribou meat and "king salmon," while pets dined on dog salmon.

Located 1107 air kilometres northwest of Yellowknife, Fort McPherson was named for a Hudson Bay Company trader. The settlement has been a Loucheux village since 1852 and was the home of Chief John Tetlichi, who became the first Dene member of the NWT Territorial Council in 1967, and Wally Firth, who was elected in 1972 as the first native MP. The settlement had a post office, RCMP detachment, government health centre, Indian day school, commercial radio station, Anglican and Roman Catholic missions, yet people there maintained a bush lifestyle until well into the sixties.

Khristine first met William in Inuvik in the late sixties while skiing. "He started hanging around me but I didn't really like him at first," she said. "I was going out with another guy [Wilbert Firth] but he kept after me."

When they finally began to go out in 1974, they seemed to click right away. She thought their marriage would, too. "At first, everything was hunky dory," Khristine said, thinking back to the early days of their marriage. "I thought everything was going to be OK."

Khristine enjoyed living in the bush. Even though you could only get into Old Crow by plane, she found that charming. She liked catching and preparing fish for dinner and drying animal skin.

Eight months into the marriage, however, things began to fall apart. "At first it was mostly jealousy," she said. "He was very possessive. Towards the end I wasn't allowed to walk up to the store without telling him how long I would be gone."

The dark-haired woman with round, pudgy features put all her trust in William, 23, who was away two weeks of every month working on the rigs. He would spend only one week at home and that usually consisted of seven days of constant nagging and arguing.

On first inspection, William seemed the awesome, perfect male. At 2 metres in height, he probably attracted more attention from women than he could handle. A closer look, however, revealed a man who had the packaging but lacked in content. William was a self-absorbed, self-centred man who needed control.

Soon Khristine discovered that it was her husband, not she, who required surveillance. The days he wasn't at home he often spent hopping from one bed to another, in Inuvik, Fort McPherson or Alkavik. Khristine would get phone calls – lots of them – from women who knew what her husband was up to. "He didn't have to say anything, I knew it through phone calls," she recalled. "My friends would say 'How could you live like this?'"

Distraught and worried, Khristine would visit her husband's mother and grandmother for comfort and advice. They were suspicious of the gossip. They told her to turn a blind eye to her so-called friends. Why believe them? The person she should listen to, they said, was William.

She also enlisted the help of the community's elders. The elders gave her good, solid advice: they told her to work at her marriage. Try to do things in a calm way, they told her. "I thought there must be something wrong and I have to sort this out. But William didn't even like me talking to other people."

One evening she sat down with her husband. Calmly, she told him what she wanted: a marriage that worked, a family, things that she thought would ultimately lead them to long-lasting happiness. "How am I going to make this marriage work if you're not spending time with me?" she asked him. "You're saying you're jealous over me, yet you're not home with me."

William, however, was less than forthcoming. Finally,

in frustration, she blurted out: "If we can't work it out, why don't I just go home?" That's when she suggested they have a trial separation. At least with time off, they could sort out what was important.

"He said it was completely out of the question so we decided to think it over and see if we're going to make it."

Khristine thought it over and naively decided perhaps a baby might put their marriage on track. "However, when I had a baby, things got worse, not better," she recalled. "And eventually I started drinking."

The arguments between husband and wife became violent. "I would wake up with a broken rib or two black eyes or a broken arm," she said. Even before her baby was born, William would knock her to the ground and kick her.

"I didn't go out and screw around like he does so he had to take his guilty conscience somewhere," she said, adding that he constantly accused her of sleeping around on him.

Two weeks before her due date, Khristine had to fly to Inuvik, the hospital where most women from Old Crow gave birth. Since William was working on the house, her sister, Louise, decided to accompany her.

While in Inuvik, the pair decided to go to a bar. They sat there chatting when Louise said she had to go to the washroom. As she walked to the ladies' room, a woman sitting at the bar noticed the stitching on the back of Louise's jacket. It said "Old Crow." The young woman, who looked like a "slut," according to Khristine, approached their table.

"She asked me if I knew William Linklater," she recalled. Khristine replied that she knew him quite well, but didn't elaborate. The woman then asked Khristine if she could give him a message and Khristine nodded her head yes. "Tell him I'll be in town if he wants to look me up," she purred before walking away.

Louise returned to the table to find Khristine white with rage. "What's the matter with you?" she asked. Khristine relayed the story, trying to control her anger. "Why didn't you just give her a good sock in the face?" Louise asked.

The upsetting conversation pushed her into an early labour. Three days later, on October 10, 1976, she gave birth to a boy whom she named Norman Linklater. This miracle seemed to fill her with enough joy that she felt she could overlook her swivel-headed husband.

However, the instant she stepped off the plane in Old Crow, she couldn't help but pass the "message" on. After showing him her newborn son, she told William that a "slut" wanted him to know she was in Inuvik if he was so inclined. "I told him the message and he said, 'I don't believe you.'"

Although William "loved his little boy," the fighting continued and increased in intensity. Six months later, Khristine told herself enough was enough. She packed up her baby, her belongings and took a flight home to Fort McPherson. Crying but determined, she told her mother the story of William's infidelities, temper and his constant barrage of insults and beatings.

"I told them I'm not going back and I will raise my son

by myself," she said. "In those days, divorce was a no-no. They told me you've got to work it out." Khristine dug in her heels and said her mind was made up. Finally, patience gave way to frustration and she yelled: "Look at me. A week later, I'll be in bed with a big, black eye."

Upon finding his wife and child gone, William became distraught. "One of his brothers called me and said he really freaked out," she recalled. "The whole family was on my case. They were feeling sorry for William instead of feeling sorry for me and my son."

The family pressure proved more than Khristine could bear and she felt her resolve starting to break down. A knock at the door confirmed the worst. It was William, playing the jilted man to the hilt. He looked frazzled and he cried instantly upon setting eyes on the wife and son who had abandoned him.

"He started crying to me," she recalled. "He said 'it's not going to be like that.'" With that, she packed up her child and their things and went back home to what turned out to be the same old soap opera.

Only now it was getting uglier. Khristine was being beaten regularly. William couldn't handle the fact she was spending so much time with the baby. Although he said he loved Norman, he couldn't stand what he saw as his wife's divided love. The beatings grew as monotonous as her hatred for the man who fathered her infant, built her the house and was the unrelenting chauvinist who openly discussed his double-standard.

For the entire summer of 1978, Khristine felt she was getting "signals" from animals that danger was looming in her life but she didn't pay close attention. Once she came upon a moose that had crashed down onto the grass after being shot. "I went over to it because I was going to skin it and it lunged up at me," she said.

Another time, she was fetching water from the Porcupine River for an old woman when she noticed two wolves, one black, the other grey, growling and snarling at her. Khristine ran to get a gun. By the time she returned, they were out of sight.

She ignored these portents. A week later, on the evening of August 31, 1978, serious trouble erupted as Khristine, a neighbour, Esther Lord, and William drank nearly three bottles of whisky. Khristine said she really didn't want to drink but was coaxed into it by her husband. Details after that are murky. Apparently, at one point, Khristine was outside and William was kicking her. Then she went back inside the cabin and passed out on the bed.

She subsequently awoke during the early hours of September 1 and began to feed the baby. William made a slighting remark about her ability to care for the child. He said she better smarten up and look after their nine-month-old son properly or there'd be trouble. Care? Khristine cared with all her heart. William's snide remark drove her into a rage. She took down a high-powered .30-.30 rifle from the wall, grabbed the shells and took off after him, seething: "If I can't kill him, I'll kill myself."

She caught up with her husband by the airstrip that had brought Old Crow so much destruction. Five shots were heard and William, wearing a blue-denimed jacket and jeans, stumbled into a ditch. Khristine was standing 250 metres away, a dazed look on her face.

The gun was still in her right hand, its barrel resting at her side. She stared vacantly at the solitary figure splayed on the runway. He looked grotesquely deformed: part of his head was missing.

Suddenly, the high-pitched voice of her brother-in-law snapped her out of her daydream state. He yelled at her to hand over the gun. Before she could react, an RCMP officer grabbed her from behind. In seconds, he had the weapon and prisoner in his grasp.

The petite Indian woman tried to haul herself in front of a plane that was landing but the Mountie held onto her tight. So desperately sad, she didn't realize there was nothing to fight about anymore. William, the husband, father, wife-beater and philanderer, was dead.

The officer frisked Khristine and found packages of shells inside her pant pockets. It was almost enough ammunition to kill the entire community of Old Crow. Today, at age 36, Khristine can make light of it. "I don't remember bringing that much ammunition with me but I guess I did."

Khristine was taken into custody, fingerprinted, photographed and charged with the first-degree murder. To lay that charge, police had to believe the killing of William was planned and deliberate.

Little did she know the story of how she was pushed to kill would touch an entire nation and prompt a crusade of women, lawyers and a Toronto journalist to do everything possible to stop the courts from punishing a woman whose life with her husband had been punishment enough.

After an investigation and a preliminary hearing in March 1979, the police flew Khristine to Whitehorse to stand trial, leaving her child with her mother-in-law in Old Crow.

Hundreds of kilometres away in Whitehorse, an all-white jury of three elderly women and three men was selected for the trial. The jurors heard that while the legal level of alcohol impairment in the Yukon was .08 mg of alcohol in 100 mL of blood, Khristine's count that day – hours after she finished drinking – was .19 mg of alcohol in 100 mL of blood. To this day, Khristine still doesn't have a clear picture of what occurred. "It's still very foggy."

What hurt Linklater's case most, though, was her refusal to speak to the all-white jury about William's violent behaviour – a refusal that surprised her lawyer, Bruce Willis of Whitehorse. Instead, she chose to testify on the facts of her case. There was a reason for this: before the trial, a brother of William's turned up drunk at the jail. He warned her she'd be punished if she got off easy and she had better not blacken William Linklater's name. Throughout the trial, Linklater's four brothers sat in the front row, glowering at a visibly upset Khristine.

Not surprisingly, the jury had less than a total picture to deal with. They knew nothing of the hell she had had to pay for living a battered existence. After three hours of deliberation, the jury returned March 15, 1979, finding her guilty of second-degree murder with a life sentence and no eligibility of parole for 10 years. The bulk of her sentence would be served in Kingston, Ont. in the Prison for Women, commonly referred to as P4W by female inmates. A gasp went up in the courtroom at the verdict.

Social workers, women and other citizens in the North who knew the whole story also were disgusted with the verdict. A mention of it in *The Toronto Star* prompted Sunday feature writer Frank Jones to hop a plane to Whitehorse to get the story. His articles sparked dozens of people across the country to help. Women wrote letters to newspapers discussing their lives with their battering husbands in what was the unspoken crime of the north.

Prominent civil rights lawyer Clayton Ruby offered his assistance, as did a wealthy long-time friend of Jones who had had her own share of searing tragedies. The woman, who asked to remain anonymous, offered to pay $5,000 for Khristine to be flown four thousand kilometres to Toronto to take alcoholism treatment at the Donwood Institute.

Back in Whitehorse, Khristine's new lawyer, Paul O'Brien, gave notice of an appeal and made an application for bail while Jones looked for accommodation for Khristine before she was admitted into the Donwood. If no one else came forward, Jones offered to take her into his Toronto home. Mr. Justice Harry Madison, faced with an anonymous assistance of financial help, took a risk and named Jones as Khristine's guardian upon her release. A successful community drive by a Whitehorse civil servant and a local minister raised bail for Khristine, who was released in Jones' custody. She stayed with his family for a month until she moved into the Donwood Institute.

Jones, now a *Toronto Star* columnist and an author, described Khristine as a very engaging person. Looking back, he thought Khristine had a lot of hope for the future. "She was so well-motivated and seemed so well-equipped to do something with her life," he said later in an interview.

After her stint at the Donwood, she was placed in custody at the Toronto Detention Centre for eight months and two native Indian residences, Anduhyaun and the Pedahbun Lodge treatment centre where counsellor Don Girard gave her support pending her appeal.

During her wait, she met a young Indian from the Orillia area who proposed marriage. She conceived a girl, Janine, while she was living in the Indian residence. She started making plans to become a heavy equipment operator in the Yukon and to complete her Grade 12 education through correspondence. (She turned down the marriage proposal, saying she wouldn't be ready for that for another four or five years). She wrote poems, which she signed "Springflower." One such poem contained these words:

> I feel no pain, no longing to hear
> Good news or bad news
> For in my mind I control
> The silence of time, and closed doors
> Set me free at heart.

During her stay in Toronto, Jones said there were times that Khristine gave him pause. Once he was called in the middle of the night after Khristine had "gone off boozing" while staying at Anduhyaun Indian women's residence.

Meanwhile, on the legal front things were looking up. During a two-day hearing before a three-member appeal panel, O'Brien cited 11 alleged flaws in the original charging of trial judge J.G. Ruttan. On November 20, 1980, in a 56-page judgment, appeal court Justice W.A. Craig substituted a verdict of manslaughter instead of second-degree murder. Khristine was handed a suspended sentence. Probation conditions included that she behave properly and not consume alcohol.

Khristine was elated. She could see her son, now age 3, whom she hadn't laid eyes on for more than two years. He had been staying with her mother-in-law in Old Crow. She looked forward to finally being able to plan a life. "I thank God that I met the Jones family," she said later.

Although Khristine Linklater may have been ready for her return north, many of its citizens weren't ready for her. Khristine said that at first she couldn't cope with the knowledge that she had killed a man, and spent most of her time alone. "I knew what I did was very wrong but at the same time I couldn't forgive myself."

As she strolled through Fort McPherson, some brash residents called her murderer to her face. "That's what I couldn't accept, you know," she said. "The first time someone called me a murderer I started beating up on them because I didn't know how to deal with it."

Khristine said part of her problem is that she never sat down with a psychiatrist or social worker to fully exorcise her guilt over the killing of her husband.

Not even God could give her forgiveness for what she had done, she said. "I couldn't even ask Him at that time." Now an Anglican, at that time she said she didn't want to ask because she thought she would never go to heaven.

Unable to cope, Khristine got into fistfights with men and women at drinking parties. "I had a guilty conscience and my feelings were hurt and I didn't know how to accept it," she said. "The only way I knew how to deal with it is to punch somebody out."

Within 18 months, she was charged with assault causing bodily harm, failing to appear, and breach of probation. In April 1982, she was sentenced to 16 months for these offences to be served in a Whitehorse jail. It was an enormous setback. The sentencing judge told Linklater the high hopes the court had for her rehabilitation had not been realized and she "had fallen by the wayside without much explanation."

The new sentence also prompted the Whitehorse Crown attorney's office to apply for Khristine to be resentenced on the manslaughter charge. Despite arguments from Linklater's lawyer, Eloise Spitzer, that retroactive sentencing for manslaughter would be unconstitutional, Deputy Yukon Supreme Court Justice John Ruttan overturned the earlier suspended sentence and sent her to Whitehorse prison for three years.

The thought of spending three years behind bars

enraged and frightened Linklater. "I thought, 'I'm going to commit suicide.' I thought there must be something wrong with me," she said. "I kept thinking of ways to kill myself and how am I going to do it this time."

She was especially embarrassed at letting down all those people who had tried so hard to help her. All that effort, expense and work by dozens seemed to be all for naught because she screwed up. But she got some good counselling – from social workers who worked out of the jail – and from Wilbert Firth, who had been a boyfriend before her marriage to William.

"He kept telling me that's not the way to deal with things," she said. "And I finally started listening." She stopped jumping to conclusions and being so defensive. During the two years Khristine spent in the Whitehorse prison, she became the spokeswoman for a group of female inmates seeking better conditions, training, and counselling. "I started changing things and I felt better."

Clayton Ruby said Khristine's troubles after leaving Toronto could have been predicted. "No social services were made available to her and then she is sent back home. You can't expect her to change alone." Frank Jones, however, was very disappointed in her, as well as with himself. "I was a little bit cynical. Unfortunately, she turned out to be what the justice system said she was – prone to violence." But her lawyer, Paul O'Brien in Whitehorse, saw it differently. "It took her another lesson to teach her she had to get her life organized," he said later. "She had to make up her mind to succeed."

Released on parole in 1984, Kristine took up with

Wilbert Firth, whom she married on April 23, 1988. "It took me two years to make up my mind and marry him. We talked and talked it out," she said. "But it changed my whole outlook."

Now, Khristine seems finally able to forgive and forget. "There's nothing I can do about him [William] anymore. "Wilbert wants to be the father of Janine. He wanted the two of us. He wanted a life for us. It's married life. I enjoy being his wife. It's the first time I've been happy in a long time."

Although it was a long road to recovery, Khristine says most of it is due to her husband. "I really admire him, he really opened me up a lot more. I wanted somebody who I was able to trust." They have two girls living with them, Janine, 10, and Kayla, 6, Wilbert's natural daughter. Her son Norman, 14, currently lives with her mother-in-law in Old Crow. The couple works in Fort McPherson, she as a land-use planning coordinator and he as a land claims coordinator. "I am hoping to get my own outfitting business one day," she said recently.

More than ever, Khristine realizes how important it is to be in touch with her spiritual self – something she has learned from the elders and her Christian faith. "I read the Bible every day and I still talk to the elders. They teach me the customs and ways of our land." "Once every three or four years, it [the killing] will hit me all of a sudden. When that happens, I learn to read the Bible more."

FIVE

Baby on a Bus

IT WAS late in the afternoon of St. Patrick's Day, 1985. Janitor William Downey Corbin was rushing around the garage of the Halifax bus terminal, looking for a plunger. After a fruitless search, he grabbed a copper "snake" and proceeded to the women's washroom to see if he could fix the clogged toilet a dispatcher had complained about. When he arrived at the stall and peered inside, he knew at once what the problem was. Resting in the base of the toilet bowl was, as he succinctly put it, "a gob of afterbirth."

Corbin had experience in these matters. After all, he had seen his wife give birth. This particular afterbirth was floating in a sea of blood. After prodding it with the metal rod, he raised it out of the toilet and shook it into a garbage can. After flushing the toilet three or four times, he then walked over to his boss, Bob Beverley, the dispatcher of Acadian Bus Lines, to tell him he had "better notify the city police or the detectives."

Within minutes, detectives and identification officers of the Halifax police department were on the scene. While they were investigating and photographing the detritus in the garbage can, William Dwayne Mac-Donald, another employee of Acadian, was making his own discovery in the garage.

MacDonald lined up bus #103 to the dump hole in the terminal. While emptying out the portable steel toilet from the outside, he noticed a wave of blood spurt from the toilet pipe. However, he didn't pay too much attention and began to hose the inside of the tank with water. Since the bus toilet was plugged, he reported it to the dispatcher but no one at the time thought much of it.

The following day Myles Hutt, another Acadian employee, was cleaning up that same bus from the inside, when he noticed "blood and stuff" on the aluminum toilet seat. Hutt had earlier been instructed by his supervisor to put the bus in the washing bay because the police were coming down to inspect all vehicles that had come into the depot. If he had time, he should try to unclog the toilet, the supervisor told Hutt.

When Hutt went to the toilet, he noticed it wasn't filled with its usual five gallons of blue chemical liquid. Inserting a pipe normally used to remove pop cans and other objects, he felt "something soft." Looking into the toilet, Hutt saw that the "something" was an infant boy with dirty-blonde matted hair, laying on its left side, with a fluorescent-looking blue umbilical cord jutting more than 13 cm from his stomach. A dark blue ink – likely the toilet chemical – stained his legs, the left side of the body and his left arm. He was a big, beefy-looking child with a flat-looking, stiff face.

Detective Obrey Benjamin of the Halifax police had inspected the mystery placenta on March 17. Now, along with officer Lloyd Williams and police photographer Danny Young, he was being asked to investigate the appearance of a dead baby. Entering the bus, he walked to the washroom at its rear where he "observed a newborn baby in the bottom of the toilet."

Benjamin instructed Young to take pictures of the infant. After this was done, Benjamin stripped off his jacket and brought the baby out of the bowl and laid him on the toilet seat. Arrangements were made for the body removal people to take the remains to the pathology lab.

Not surprisingly, the discovery garnered considerable media attention. "Dead Baby Found in Bus Bathroom," shouted a headline from *The Daily News,* a Halifax tabloid. The March 19 front-page story stated that, "A newborn baby was found dead Monday after an attempt to flush his body down a toilet on an Acadian Lines bus yesterday. The baby was found at 8:15 a.m. yesterday by an employee cleaning the bus washroom. Halifax police are searching for the mother, who is believed to have been on the bus which arrived at the Almon St., Halifax terminal from Sydney late Sunday afternoon." The story finished with a plea to any one of the 47 bus passengers who left Sydney that Sunday at 9:45 a.m. and arrived in Halifax at 3:15 p.m. to contact police.

Police were of the opinion that whomever had given birth to the infant had deliberately flushed it down the toilet to kill it. They were supported in their assessment by Dr. Roland Perry, Nova Scotia's chief medical examiner, who, after an autopsy on March 18, concluded that the boy's umbilical cord appeared to have been cut.

With the release of the public appeal, calls started to pour into police headquarters. One of the most promising leads came from an anonymous tipster who said the dead baby's suspected mother was one Cheryl Lynn Tutty, 21, a home economics student at Mount St. Vincent University. The tipster described what she was wearing the day the baby was found.

On March 27, Detective Benjamin went to Mount St. Vincent to make inquiries as to Tutty's whereabouts. He was told she lived with an older sister at 14 Melody Drive in Rockingham, close to the university. Greeting Benjamin at the Melody Drive apartment was a pleasant-looking blonde. Yes, I'm Cheryl Tutty, she acknowledged under questioning, not the least bit evasive. She explained that, yes, she had been pregnant but had delivered the baby in St. Rita's hospital in Sydney during the weekend and had given it up for adoption. Benjamin went back to the station and called the hospital where she said she had the infant. Hospital officials said they had no such record of the birth.

With a search warrant in hand, Benjamin went back to the Tutty apartment, this time with Constable Dave Ross, also of Halifax Police. Cheryl wasn't there so he talked to her sister. Charlene Tutty said she didn't know Cheryl had been pregnant. True, she had noticed her sister had gained weight around the stomach, but she had gained 7 kg every university year herself. "It's just a family trait."

She tried to reach her sister over the telephone, without success. Benjamin then showed her the search warrant and outlined what he was looking for: a blue coat, a pair of sweat pants, sneakers and a grey purse. She pointed to the bedroom. He grabbed the coat from the closet, the sweatpants, which had been folded with some clean clothes on the dresser, and her shoes. Charlene provided a plastic bag in which to put the seized articles. Just as Benjamin was taking Charlene Tutty's statement, Cheryl Lynn Tutty walked through the door.

The detective informed Tutty that he had seized some of her clothing and that she was under arrest. She was read the standard police caution and told she would have an opportunity to contact a lawyer once she went downtown with police. She was then taken to the department's criminal investigation bureau where, at 10:45 a.m., she gave a statement to Constable David Ross and another officer.

Ross asked if Tutty would like to see a doctor. Yes, she would. And a minister, too. As she signed her statement, she felt the need to explain the tragedy. "Because I wasn't seeing a doctor, I didn't know when I was due and actually thought I had a few more weeks before having the baby."

Police took Tutty to the Victoria General Hospital's emergency department, where she complained to Dr. Janet Elizabeth McNaughton of dizziness and lightheadedness, particularly when standing. Tutty identified herself as "the girl who had the baby on the bus." She explained she had had the infant 10 days ago and had not received any medical supervision or prenatal care before or after the birth.

McNaughton did a pelvic examination and checked Tutty's overall health. After doing some blood tests, it was determined that Tutty was suffering from anemia, referred to medically as a low haemoglobin. It was strictly from a lack of iron, the doctor confirmed. Otherwise Tutty was fine.

Cheryl Lynn Tutty's trauma had begun almost two weeks earlier. On March 15 she was at the Halifax airport, anxiously waiting for a plane to take her to her parents and son in Louisbourg, in Nova Scotia's Cape Breton region. Her mother, Mabel, father, William, and some of her other nine siblings were going to celebrate the first birthday of her son, Jason.

Born March 13, 1984, Jason was a "love-child." Tutty had become pregnant with him during her first year of university and now Tutty's parents were raising him at their Cape Breton home until his mother completed her bachelor of science degree in home economics. Tutty commuted to Cape Breton almost every weekend to see Jason.

What Cheryl's relatives hadn't noticed for the past eight months was that she was pregnant. Again. Tutty didn't show much, however, she made a point of wearing baggy clothing. Ashamed that she had made the same "mistake" twice – this time with a different man – Tutty couldn't bring herself to tell her parents. Nor did she seek prenatal care.

Tears streamed down Cheryl Tutty's face as she waited for her plane. She had asked Bruce Boyd Kennedy, the father-to-be, to drive her to the airport that weekend but he had refused. She had started seeing Kennedy, a tall black-haired young man who attended Dalhousie University in Halifax, in the summer of 1983 in Louisbourg. They had been friends for 10 years and their relationship at first was an on-again, off-again affair. It wasn't until the summer of 1984 that it became more "serious." That's when she got pregnant. Tutty and Kennedy discussed the options that seemed available – abortion, adoption, raising the child on his or her own – but as the months passed, no action was taken to resolve the matter.

The birthday weekend in Louisbourg passed without Tutty's parents discovering her condition. Back in Halifax, Tutty called on Kennedy at his apartment in Bedford, outside of the city. Kennedy told her he was just on his way to the Chicken Chalet and asked if she'd like to go. As they walked there, Tutty told Kennedy that "she had had the baby in Sydney Saturday morning – Friday night, Saturday morning, whatever." He showed little curiosity about the baby, or Tutty, declining to enquire about what hospital Tutty went to, where the baby was, or how Tutty had coped. Later he would remember "she didn't look that bad."

After their chat, she stayed at his apartment that night. The following day, he went to school.

Ten days later the mother of his child was behind bars.

Following her arrest, Tutty tried to hire a lawyer, eventually ending up with Joel Pink, one of the Maritimes' top counsellors, and a man who would later defend another accused female killer, Lisa MacDonald, (see *Love and Death*).

Later that evening, Tutty was placed in a police lineup where Bernie Peter Chaisson, a passenger on the March 17 Sydney-to-Halifax bus, identified her. Cheryl Lynn Tutty's fate seemed sealed.

The youngest of 10 children, she was raised in a fairly strict household. Mabel Tutty wouldn't let her children stay out late at night – they all had curfews. Every Sunday, the family would head to St. Bartholomew's, the local Anglican church in Louisbourg, to sing and say their prayers.

In short, historic Louisbourg and Tutty's parents seemed to offer Cheryl a quiet, stable, interesting environment in which to grow up. There was skating and hockey. Cheryl joined the Girl Guides, took babysitting courses at the suggestion of her mother, and loved playing volleyball at school. Each one of the Tutty children had an assigned chore around the house, be it dishes or mending torn clothes.

William, the father, was at times very distant. A quiet man who worked as a plumber, he found it difficult to engage in conversation and instead concentrated on listening. He compensated for his withdrawn disposition by helping his children with school projects.

Since they had little money, the family had to be frugal. What vacations they took were spent by taking some children to friend's homes in other parts of the province.

"We didn't do a whole lot of things together because there were too many of us to fit in the car," Robert Tutty, a brother three years Cheryl's senior, said in an interview. Describing Cheryl as an introvert, he said his sister was often quiet and introspective – the sibling who was most like her father. "She's as harmless as a kitten."

When Cheryl Tutty was old enough, she taught Sunday school. By her teens, she was working as a babysitter, then landed jobs in restaurants, which at first consisted of cleaning up in the kitchen. Soon, she worked herself up to "laying out buffets," Mabel recalled. "Her boss was very pleased with her work."

As her children grew older, Mabel Tutty stressed the value of education. She knew jobs were few and far between in the Maritimes, which traditionally has the highest unemployment in the country. "I said you can either work at the fish plant or go back to school," she recalled. It wasn't a difficult choice.

In the meantime, Mabel and her husband worked hard to save money and set aside what they could for their children's post-secondary education. Some, like Cheryl, had a trust fund, while others were given what could be spared as the academic year approached. The children "would get summer jobs, save their money and apply for student loans," Mabel said. This effort seemed to pay off: eight of the 10 Tutty children went on to earn a university degree.

At 18, Tutty packed her bags to study home economics at Mount St. Vincent. Eager to start a career, not a family, her dream was to become a dietitian. The summer after her first year of school, however, she got pregnant. Blessed with a supportive mother, Tutty managed to carry the infant through to term and give it to her parents to care for until she completed school. "They were very good with her at the university," Mabel recalled. "They still let her do her exams and she didn't get behind in school."

Mabel Tutty, who had been raised a Catholic, was deeply hurt when Cheryl was accused of being a baby-killer. She loved her daughter and certainly would have accepted a second baby in the Tutty household. "I just felt very upset that she couldn't tell me," she said.

Although the family stuck by Tutty, the father had a tough time of it. "He couldn't go up to the trial at all. He just couldn't deal with it," Mabel said. "He said we could have taken in another one [baby]."

People, of course, gossiped but "most of them were good," Mabel noted. The only really upsetting incident in the months leading up to the trial occurred when RCMP officers from New Brunswick came knocking at the Tutty's door. An abandoned baby had been discovered and they wanted Mabel to account for her daughter's whereabouts. Well, "there was no blessed way she was in that province," she recalled telling them. "Besides, she wouldn't have had time to carry the baby."

Charged with second-degree murder, Cheryl Tutty first had to face a preliminary hearing to determine if there was enough evidence to bring her to trial. Eighteen Crown witnesses were heard at the April hearing including Dr. Roland Perry, the chief medical examiner.

Although Perry had considerable public support in a province where one third of the population is Catholic, his testimony in support of the murder charge was harmed by one crucial fact: he was not a pathologist.

In his autopsy report, Perry had described the baby, known only as Infant Male Tutty, as well-developed, with the "appearance of a full-term infant." He weighed 3 kg, was 48 m from head to heel and was well-nourished. Rigor mortis had completely set in. After examining the placenta, Perry said it weighed .6 kg and had an attached umbilical cord. He said the placenta was consistent with belonging to a full-term baby. The far edge of the 14 cm long cord had the appearance of being cut.

Tutty's attorney, however, argued to Provincial Court Judge William J.C. Atton that Perry had no qualifications as a pathologist nor any expertise in umbilical cords to give expert opinion as to the severing of one. Said Joel Pink: "I will be objecting to Dr. Perry, if your honour pleases, giving any evidence as to how in fact that cord was severed, unless my learned friend can so qualify him as a pathologist. I would respectfully submit to the court that he is not qualified to give this type of evidence. He's a medical doctor and a medical examiner."

Perry explained to the judge that, as medical examiner, he not only determines the cause of death but interprets wounds. He had been a medical examiner, part-time, since 1964 and full-time since 1977. In that time, he had performed 3,000 autopsies on victims of shootings, stabbings, hangings, and strangulation. "I have in fact 21 years of experience in seeing this type of thing," Perry declared. "And I certainly am able to determine what is a cut as opposed to what is a laceration in a great majority of cases."

Under cross-examination, however, Perry admitted that he had never been called upon to say whether an umbilical cord has been cut or ruptured, had never read up on ruptured cords, precipitated deliveries, or the tension strength of cords.

Perry proved a tough witness. Just answering a question succinctly didn't seem to be enough for him and the judge frequently had to cut in. Perry seemed hurt, if not offended, that his abilities were being challenged.

Ruling on the validity of Perry's expertise, Judge Atton made Joel Pink a happy man. "Dr. Perry's evidence, in my opinion, in relation to the cause of the severing of the umbilical cord, is not accepted by me as an expert opinion on that. I don't think he can go any further than any other practitioner who comes in and says that the wound is, in his opinion, consistent with a cut or that it appeared to have been, it was a smooth severing rather than a jagged severing."

After that, Perry picked up where he left off and informed the jury of his other findings. Apart from a four-centimetre scratch, there were no signs of injury. The brain was mushy in appearance. "As a result of the examinations, my opinion [is] that this was a full-term infant capable of independent existence, [who] had in fact, breathed on its own and died as a result of asphyxia, which is basically the lack of oxygen combined with a lack of the ability to get rid of carbon dioxide," he said.

Judge Atton didn't seem to buy this, however. In his ruling he declared that he didn't "think that there is sufficient evidence for committal of Miss Tutty on the evidence which was presented here for the charge as laid."

With that extremely unpopular finding, Cheryl Lynn Tutty was dismissed. Judge Atton, of course, was perfectly correct in his ruling because there was absolutely no physical evidence to prove Tutty had cut the umbilical cord and purposely flushed the child down the toilet — what was needed to constitute a second-degree murder charge.

On April 29, the Attorney General's department issued a stay of proceedings and cancelled the trial date that had been set to begin May 5. However, in a highly unusual move, the Attorney General of Nova Scotia, Ron Giffin, personally preferred a bill of indictment and pushed the case to trial. Once again, Cheryl Tutty was charged with second-degree murder and neglecting to obtain assistance in child birth.

An angry Joel Pink went to the Supreme Court of Nova Scotia to block it, arguing the indictment was an infringement on his client's constitutional rights. "The applicant alleges a breach of the accused's right not to be left dangling on the hook of an unsubstantiated criminal charge; that a favorable decision after a preliminary inquiry should be determinitive of her innocence and that a preferred indictment infringes her right to be presumed innocent. Clearly the right to life is not the legal right involved in this case."

However, a written decision released June 9, 1986,

Chief Justice Constance Glube said that the Attorney General was not vexatious or abusive and the preferred bill of indictment did not offend the presumption of innocence. Concluded Glube: "The preferring of an indictment by the Attorney General is demonstrably justified as a reasonable limit prescribed by law in a free and democratic society."

And so it came to pass that on June 23, 1986, Cheryl Lynn Tutty stood trial for the second-degree murder of Infant Male Tutty. Jury selection was surprisingly brief after many prospective jurors – obviously not eager to serve on the panel – failed to show up. After 20 minutes, a five-woman, seven-man jury was selected from a sample of 42 residents. Joel Pink represented Tutty, the prosecution was handled by Gary Holt.

Tutty sat in the prisoner's box. Her mother and a sister, Beverley, were in the audience, ready to support her. They sat and responded without emotion to the medical evidence and graphic photographs that were entered into evidence.

In the prosecution's opening address, Crown attorney Holt said he would be calling 20 witnesses – six medical doctors among them – who would testify that Infant Male Tutty had been born alive and that his umbilical cord had been severed.

Constable Danny Young of Halifax police was one of the first witnesses to testify. Most of his testimony concentrated on presenting diagrams of the bus, the interior washroom, a schematic diagram of the mechanics of the toilet the baby was found in, and the admission of two plastic vials of Tutty's blood into evidence.

Admitted as well were Tutty's blue, three-quarter length coat, a pair of light blue sneakers, blue sweat pants, and her purse. A blue-flowered seat cover that Tutty stained on the bus was also presented. There were also vivid, colour photographs of the infant, with his matted hair and stained body. In some pictures, he is laying on his side, on others he is face up. In many, he is laying in the toilet bottom.

More than a dozen witnesses testified during the first day. There was Karen Martin, an Acadian Lines ticket agent who said she went to the terminal washroom an hour after the bus from Sydney had arrived St. Patrick's Day. There, she saw a toilet filled to the brim with blood.

"There was a big blob in the toilet but I didn't know what it was," she said, adding that she got another ticket agent to look at it. Together, the two of them figured it out. "I went into the ticket office and into the back room and sat down because I was upset over what I had seen," she testified.

Georgina Muise, one of two bus passengers to testify, said she saw a young pregnant woman bent over on a bench in the Sydney terminal washroom, a woman she now believed to be Cheryl Tutty. On March 17, when the bus reached Antigonish, the halfway point between Sydney and Halifax, Muise said she saw the woman in the terminal washroom there, sitting bent over on a bench. Then the woman went into one of the washroom stalls, where she stayed for about 10 or 15 minutes. Under cross-examination by Pink, Muise said she heard no noises from the washroom and when the young woman returned to her seat, nothing was said.

The other passenger, Bernie Chaisson, told the court that he had taken the seat beside Cheryl Tutty, who was sitting on the edge of her seat, turning toward the aisle. Moments after they reached Enfield, 40 km north of Halifax, the woman walked to the bathroom at the rear of the bus, where she stayed for about 15 or 20 minutes.

During her absence, "I went to relax and all that and just laid down – just sort of leaned on my arm and when I was looking down [at Tutty's seat] it was wet." He pulled his arm away. When the woman left the bus, Chaisson said "it seemed like she was trying to conceal her behind with a bag or suitcase." Chaisson later went to the police and selected Tutty out of a lineup as being the woman on the bus. "I just walked in there and knew right away who it was."

Cross-examined by Pink, neither Muise nor Chaisson could remember Tutty bringing a purse or anything else with her to the toilet on the bus where the baby was found. It was an important question, considering there was medical evidence strongly suggesting the umbilical cord had been cut.

Tutty's former boyfriend, Bruce Boyd Kennedy, admitted under cross-examination that he was interested in Tutty getting an abortion but she had refused.

June 24 was set aside for medical evidence. Two experts testified the baby was alive and had, in fact, inhaled a few breaths of air when he was born. This would be hotly disputed by Pink.

One of the experts, Dr. Stephen Boudreau, a pathologist at the Halifax Infirmary Hospital, testified that it appeared the infant had breathed after birth as his lungs had expanded. The infant's lungs contained many gas bubbles, likely caused by the inhalation of bacteria in the toilet. To confirm his finding, Boudreau said there was a hemorrhage in the lungs, which meant the infant's heart was beating when he was born. However, under cross-examinination, Boudreau conceded those symptoms could have been caused by fetal distress and may have resulted as a death in the womb – something the mother likely would not have realized.

A second expert, Dr. Robert Jackson, head of the radiology department at the Izaak Walton Killam Hospital in Halifax, showed the jury X-rays of the baby's head, lungs, abdomen and legs. He determined that there was air in the child's lungs, stomach and upper intestine. This could only be there if the child had taken several breaths after birth.

The baby's heart was abnormally small with very little blood circulating, which suggested the infant may have bled from the umbilical cord after birth, as his heart was pumping. Bony centres in the infant's knees revealed the boy was close to term, likely 38 weeks. The baby's skull bones were not overlapped as frequently seen immediately after birth, which meant the birth occurred very rapidly, he said.

In a peculiar turn of events, Madam Justice Glube decided that chief medical examiner Dr. Roland Perry was capable of giving expert opinion evidence, after having been denied that privilege at the preliminary hearing. This prompted a strong objection from Pink who cited the previous judge's ruling that Perry, in fact, could not give expert opinion evidence on those facts.

Pink's objection was denied, however, and Perry went on to testify that the umbilical cord had been partially cut, then ripped. Under a gruelling two-hour cross-examination, he acknowledged that the cord may have ruptured through natural causes. At the same time, the outer edge of the umbilical cord was sharply demarcated, except for a slight tail on one side, which was consistent with cutting, then tearing it, he said.

As Perry spoke, Cheryl Tutty for the first time in three days, became visibly emotional, wiping tears from her eyes.

Perry admitted to Pink he didn't examine the umbilical cord under a microscope and could not say whether it might have ruptured from inflammation or varicose veins. He acknowledged, too, that he hadn't read a 1983 pathology report which stated the edges of an umbilical cord could be smooth even if torn and not cut.

Another expert witness for the prosecution, Dr. Ernest Cutz, senior staff pediatric pathologist at the Hospital for Sick Children in Toronto, supported some of Perry's conclusions. He agreed the infant breathed after birth and found bacteria, meat fibres from feces and paper or cotton fibres in the boy's lungs. "The only way these things got into the baby's lungs was by the active process of inhalation and is consistent with what is found in a toilet tank," he said. "It's not possible for it to get in after he died."

However, Cutz was inconclusive as to whether the

umbilical cord was cut or had ruptured. While a rupture was rare, it could happen in a precipitate or rapid delivery. In precipitate labour, the cervix could fully dilate in one hour in a woman having her second or third child.

Pink called Dr. Stephen Allen Heifetz, a pathologist at the Izaak Walton Killam Hospital who specializes in umbilical cords, to the stand. Pink described Heifetz as one of the three top umbilical experts in the world. What an amazing stroke of luck it was to have such a specialist right in the city where the incident occurred, he said.

Heifetz indeed had an impressive list of qualifications. A graduate of New York State University, he became a member of the American Board of Pathology in 1977 and practised at U.S. Army hospitals and West Germany. He was appointed to the Department of Pediatric Pathology at the Armed Forces Institute of Pathology in Washington, D.C. where he later became chairman of that department. In June 1985, he moved to Halifax to work as a pathologist at Izaak Walton Killam and at the Grave Maternity Hospital. He was also an associate professor of pathology at Dalhousie University Medical School.

Heifetz said he had no doubt that a spontaneous rupture occurred as the baby fell into the toilet. He believed the birth occurred exactly as Tutty had explained it. A precipitate delivery – one of excessive force and speed following a labour of less than three hours – can cause the umbilical cord to rupture spontaneously. "This can occur not only when the mother is standing up to deliver the child or sitting down and delivering the child as in this case, but even when the mother is lying down, the expulsive force of the delivery may be so great as to cause the fetus to be violently expelled from the uterus with a spontaneous rupture of the cord."

Quoting from medical research, he said in one-third of the cases where there was a precipitious birth, a spontaneous rupture of an umbilical cord occurred. Heifetz disagreed with several of Perry's findings, including the medical examiner's contention that the infant was born alive. He said measuring a child's body or weighing it is not a scientifically precise way of determining whether an infant is full-term or not. Heifetz, who had attended 5,000 autopsies of newborns, said it is very rare for the infant's liver to produce red blood cells after 37 weeks. In this case, the liver was still doing this job. Tutty's baby was, in fact, only 32 to 34 weeks of age, and definitely having difficulty getting oxygen because of the large amount of amniotic fluid found in his lungs.

While he agreed with Perry that the baby died of asphyxia, Heifetz said this lack of oxygen began before birth and continued afterwards. The baby died within minutes of falling into the toilet, he said. "I am convinced from my examination of the evidence as presented to me that the story of the events of that day as told by Ms. Tutty are substantially correct. It is my belief that this child was approximately one month premature and there is substantial evidence to that effect within the report. I believe that the child was of sufficient weight and the cord was of appropriate length, such that expulsion of the child while seated on the toilet seat would have resulted in spontaneous rupture of the umbilical cord, and I believe that there is strong evidence that the child was, in fact, in deep trouble while still within the mother's womb and that there is a likelihood that the child was in fact still-born rather than live-born."

Another Killam pathologist, Dr. Paul E. Wakely, testified that the baby was premature, likely between 34 and 35 weeks of age. He determined this by examining the kidney. He also said it was highly unlikely that the child breathed air.

It was good evidence from two very convincing, highly-qualified medical doctors who appeared to make determinations using precise, scientific methods.

Later, however, Dr. Gregory Thompkins, head of the gynecology department at the Halifax Infirmary, described precipitate delivery as the "explosive, uncontrolled expulsion of the baby through the birth canal." As an obstetrician for 31 years, he had seen only two cases of rapid delivery where the umbilical cord spontaneously ruptured. Both of these occurred in a hospital where each woman was lying down. In one of them, the infant landed on the floor. He said he has heard of five cases where women gave birth into a toilet and three of those babies survived the experience.

Following the medical evidence, the "star" of the trial, Cheryl Lynn Tutty, went "on stage" on June 27.

Now 22, she told the court she had celebrated her son's first birthday in Louisbourg on March 16 and was returning to her Halifax apartment March 17 by bus. Tutty counted the weeks and figured she was due after the second week on April. When she got on the bus, she said she felt a little tired, but she was fine otherwise.

Soon, however, she felt pain in her back and abdomen

– something she at first attributed to the bumpy ride. Feeling queasy and faint, she went to the washroom at the scheduled stop in Antigonish. By this time she was having light contractions. Nevertheless, she returned to the bus. She thought she would have enough time to get to Halifax.

Near Truro, 90 km northeast of Halifax, she noted a discharge, had one strong contraction and then her water broke. Visibly upset, Tutty testified that she didn't tell anyone on the bus because she felt there still was enough time to make it to a hospital in Halifax as her contractions were five minutes apart. "I sat on the toilet and I could feel a strong contraction coming on, so I had to push to relieve the pain. Immediately after, I heard a splash. I got right up to see what had happened. I looked in the toilet but I didn't see anything in there." Then, she noticed the umbilical cord hanging from her vagina and thought she had miscarried. "Everything happened so fast and also I always thought you had to cut an umbilical cord and I hadn't done anything to this one."

She didn't call for help because she was confused and upset. Like the birth of her first child, Jason, she could not remember much about it. "I definitely did not cut the cord, I never heard the baby cry or saw the baby," she testified.

When the bus arrived in Halifax, Tutty said she went into the terminal bathroom and passed the afterbirth. After that, she took a taxi to her boyfriend's apartment to tell him she had a miscarriage.

"I never felt I had a live birth on that day. I'd like to say

I didn't want my son to die. I would have loved him as much as I love my other son, Jason. At no time did I murder my son."

Under cross-examination by Holt, Tutty said she didn't see a doctor about her pregnancy or tell her mother because it was the "second time I had made this mistake." Asked why she didn't get off the bus when she experienced labour pains, Tutty said she only had $3.

Holt: What do you think the reaction would be if you walked up to anybody in the Antigonish bus terminal and said: "I'm having a baby, help me." Would they care how much money you had?
Tutty: A taxi driver might.

Tutty had to concede that any one of the 47 other passengers on the bus would have helped her but she said she didn't feel it necessary to go to a hospital immediately because, in the case of her first child, he was born five or six hours after her water broke.

She said she didn't know what the splash was at first, but admitted it must have been the baby after she saw the cord dangling from within her. Asked why she didn't try to reach into the toilet and feel for her newborn, Tutty said: "I didn't want to see the baby because I thought I'd had a miscarriage."

Holt then asked her why she didn't contact the police after she heard radio reports about a newborn baby being found on a bus. She said she was afraid the police wouldn't believe her story. She denied that she wanted to forget about the baby forever. "I never, ever thought they wouldn't find me; I knew they would find me," she replied.

All in all, Tutty's testimony was more polished than the statement she gave to Const. David Ross shortly after her son died. Here is an excerpt from that transcript:

Ross: We are investigating a case of infanticide which occurred on an Acadian Lines bus on March 17, 1986. You do not have to say anything, do you understand that?

Tutty: Yes.

Ross: You have nothing to hope from any promise or favour and nothing to fear from any threat, whatever you do say may be written – may be given in evidence notwithstanding such promise or threat, do you understand that?

Tutty: Yes.

Ross: Do you wish to say anything?

Tutty: I realized I was pregnant about the end of September 1984. I didn't go to see a doctor. My boyfriend, Bruce Kennedy, wanted me to have an abortion, but I didn't want to have one. He was the only person who knew I was pregnant. On March 15, '85, I went to Cape Breton for the weekend to visit my parents' in Louisbourg. I flew down by E.P.A. (Eastern Provincial Airways). I left Sydney on the 17th of March, 1985, by Acadian Lines bus for Halifax. When the bus got to Antigonish, I realized I was having light contractions. After getting back on the bus in Antigonish

I thought I could make it back to Halifax before I had the baby. About Truro, I started to have really strong contractions and not long after that my water broke. I still thought I could make it to Halifax because when I had the last baby I didn't have the baby for about five hours after my water broke. I got up – got up from my seat and went to the bathroom on the bus and I just got in there and sat on the toilet and the baby came out and went right into the toilet. So I sat there for a while and got up and went to my seat. I got off the bus in Halifax and went into the bathroom and passed the afterbirth. I went and got my suitcase and changed my pants. I left by taxi and went to my boyfriend's. I didn't tell him what happened. I told him I had a miscarriage. That's it.

Ross: The coat, sweat pants, blue sneakers and purse which we took from the apartment, are they what you had on the bus on the day of the incident?

Tutty: Yes.

Ross: How did you get from the terminal to the boyfriend's?

Tutty: A taxi.

Ross: How did you cut the umbilical cord from the baby?

Tutty: I didn't cut it. I figured it just broke when the baby fell in the toilet.

Ross: How did you get to the bus Sunday morning from Louisbourg to Sydney?

Tutty: My brother William drove me.

Ross: Who knew you were pregnant?

Tutty: The only person I told was Bruce.

Following Tutty's testimony, Pink called two character witnesses to the defence. Wayne MacGree, sheriff for the county of Cape Breton, said he had known Tutty all his life and described her as an honest and truthful person.

Sister Evelyn Williams, chaplain at Mount St. Vincent University, said Tutty has a reputation around campus as a person with integrity and honesty. She is a very gentle, shy and kind person who keeps to herself, Williams said.

In his closing address, Pink urged the jury to find his client not guilty and to give "absolutely no weight" to Perry's evidence the cord had been cut. Describing Tutty as a confused lady, he said she did not call for help because she didn't know what had happened to her and she thought the baby had been stillborn. "She was a confused, upset and frightened young lady governed by the traumatic shock of the incident."

The prosecution, by contrast, questioned Tutty's professed love for her unloved child in the face of her actions. She didn't tell anyone of her pregnancy except her boyfriend, didn't consult a doctor, and didn't ask for help when the labour pains began or when the infant fell into the toilet. Tutty may not have intended in doing away with the child, but it was an unwanted pregnancy and when the opportunity arose to get rid of the baby, she took it, Gary Holt said.

"Her actions throughout caused the baby's death, although technically he died of asphyxia. If the proper actions had been taken, the child would never have landed in the toilet tank to begin with," he concluded.

After the case was wrapped up, Madame Justice Glube charged the jury for 90 minutes, explaining the five possible verdicts they could find. They were: guilty of second-degree murder, manslaughter, infanticide, concealing the body of a child, or not guity of any charge. She explained that second-degree murder and manslaughter carry sentences of life in prison while infanticide carries a maximum of five years in prison, concealing a maximum of two years.

They returned to the courtroom four times to ask for the definition of manslaughter and what constitutes an unlawful act. One hour before reaching their verdict, they asked Glube to explain the difference between manslaughter and infanticide. She told them infanticide is another form of murder which requires a specific intent to kill while manslaughter needs an unlawful act but not the intent to kill.

After deliberating for almost nine hours, the jury handed down its verdict on July 3: not guilty of second-degree murder but guilty of the lesser charge of manslaughter. Tutty was stonefaced. Pink seemed stunned; he asked that each juror be polled individually. The five women and seven men all said they agreed with the verdict.

Tutty was permitted to stay with her parents in Louisbourg for the remainder of the summer, then appeared before Madame Justice Glube on August 22, 1986 for sentencing. Pink called a psychiatrist, Dr. Edwin Rosenberg, who had met with Tutty 10 times over the past 15 months to speak at the sentencing.

Rosenberg said Tutty displayed an "adjustment

problem" to facing adulthood, noting that she showed signs of a personality disorder characterized by immaturity. She acted much younger than her 22 years. The youngest of 10 children, Tutty had told Rosenberg she felt her father favoured the sister next youngest to her. She feared getting close to people. Tutty, he said, displayed an emotional detachment from the birth process; that she had no clear plans for the infant, and that her focus was on concealing the birth.

Given her personality disorder, she needed treatment for years, not months. "I cannot say what would happen without treatment," Rosenberg said. "The difficulty of the past could be repeated." In fact, he said, it would be repeated.

The prosecution asked that a prison sentenced be imposed to deter other women from ending a pregnancy in the same way. Pink argued that his client had suffered enough, what with the trauma of childbirth, the trial and the sensational media coverage.

"The death of a child clearly cannot be condoned; and, I am not condoning what has occurred," Madame Justice Glube wrote in her judgment. "However, in my opinion…Miss Tutty did not deliberately start on that journey with the intention of having her baby on a bus." It was a case of inaction, she said. "She knows now that the child might well have lived had she obtained assistance. I would have to believe that Miss Tutty has been on an emotional roller coaster for the past period of time since she gave birth to this child and failed to get assistance…If one has to put labels on this crime then the label would be akin to accident."

In handing down a three-year suspended sentence, Glube ordered Tutty to report to a probation officer monthly, keep the peace, seek psychiatric counselling, and make a reasonable effort to find and maintain employment.

"Whether she can ever return to functioning normally in society, to earn a living and caring for her present child, will depend upon her mental strength which, with help, hopefully, will come about in time," Glube said. "I suggest to you that you will probably suffer with this for the rest of your life. But you can still be a useful member of society if in accepting the responsibility for what has occurred you then move on to ensure that you lead a productive life, accept responsibility for yourself and your actions and provide for yourself and your child."

This story had a happy ending. During the trial, Cheryl Lynn Tutty, met a supportive suitor named Michael Custance, an airplane mechanic with the Canadian Armed Forces. They married and had a son named Justin, a new brother for young Jason. The four now live in Ontario.

SIX

Twilight of the Godfather

IN 1971, a portly, dark-haired mobster named Frank Guzzo asked the father of his 18-year-old girlfriend to sign an agreement. It stated that he, Frank Guzzo, 38, of Montreal, Québec would not be prosecuted for sleeping with one Micheline Poulos in her parents' home in St. Sauveur, Québec or anywhere else. Mr. Poulos signed the document and handed it back to a satisfied Guzzo, alleviating his fears of being arrested for bedding "jail-bait."

Almost 20 years later, Micheline Poulos and Frank Guzzo were still sharing a bedroom. But on January 5, 1990, the relationship ended when Micheline Poulos took a .38-calibre handgun and fired six shots into Frank Guzzo's head. When police arrived that evening, Ms. Poulos calmly explained that Mr. Guzzo had asked for it.

Born March 8, 1953, Micheline Poulos was a non-descript, plain-looking girl who grew into a non-descript, plain-looking woman. Quiet and withdrawn, she mostly kept to herself.

Raised in a poor household in the lower Laurentians, she was the daughter and only child of a father who had difficulty establishing himself and a depressed mother who was seldom home because she was always working. On the occasions Micheline's mother was home, she didn't have time to change her child for school and rarely even faked a smile. "I don't remember [my mother] changing me in the morning or doing anything with her," Micheline would recall. "My mother always slapped me."

The Poulos family travelled all over Québec, trying to put down roots. Although Micheline's father worked hard in various businesses, success proved elusive. Still, he persisted, leaving little energy to care for the child whose solitary desire was to be loved. Home usually was a modest place. At one point, the family found themselves living in a cottage. "There was no hydro and we would wind up our line with the neighbor's for electricity. There was no hot water."

The only magic in young Micheline's life took place in a house down the street from where she lived in St. Sauveur. She passed it every day on the way to school. That home was big, a mansion, she thought. There were rich people in there and they had two children who were adopted. The kids had nice clothes, lots of toys and went on exotic trips to far-away places. They were children

who were loved; absolutely, unequivocally. Each time
Micheline passed that home she wished someone would
notice her. Maybe they would like her, too. Then she
could be part of that dream world where the tooth fairy
left a dime under the pillow. A place where stacks of pres-
ents would be placed under the Christmas tree, where
family vacations were filled with laughter. From the outside, Poulos could make out the smiling faces of the
happy children and their parents. Not once would they
see her.

As time passed, Micheline Poulos became convinced
her parents did not love her. This must be because she
wasn't worth it, she reasoned. She was nothing, a waif, a
castoff. She yearned for someone to take notice of her.
And when – or if – that someone finally did, she vowed
she would work so hard to keep that attention. She'd do
anything to just have someone tell her she's interesting,
she's important, she's pretty. For years no one did.

By the time she was 18, Micheline's father was still
trying to make a name for himself but it wasn't happening. Finally, in the early seventies, he took a job as a
chauffeur in Montreal. One of his clients was a man who
claimed to be a mobster in a city with a "rich" criminal
culture. That man was Frank Guzzo.

A jeweller by trade, Guzzo, was related by marriage to
Vincenzo "Vic" Cotroni, one of the top figures in Montreal's underworld. He had married Cotroni's only daughter, Rosina, and they had had a son, Ralph, but the marriage was a brief one, ending in divorce.

The stories of Guzzo's influence within the mob are

mixed. There are those who say he cast an almost-hyp-
notic spell on the biggest of powerbrokers, including his
father-in-law, who died in 1984. He could make them do
things they wouldn't have done for their mothers, they
say.

On the mob "flow chart," Guzzo was placed in a box
just below Vic. Yet after Guzzo's death, anti-gang members of the Montreal police force were hard-pressed to
find anything of significance about him in his file. Perhaps he had been married too short a time to build up a
power base in the Cotroni clan, and once the marriage
dissolved, he was too inconsequential to mean anything
to the mob. Guzzo, in short, seemed a lightweight, a man
who talked a good game but had no real power with anyone, anywhere. Although he had connections, they were
old ties and not necessarily strong ones.

Micheline will never forget the first time she met
Guzzo. Her parents had invited him over for dinner. Her
father served filet mignon, an expensive, tender meat she
had tasted only once before. She looked with adoration at
this man who seemed to have it all. "I thought that this
was something good. He was a man who was very elo-
quent, he spoke all night," she recalled. "I remember he
asked me that night if I was a virgin." As Micheline's
father walked him out to the car, Guzzo said: "Hurry up,
Tom, and make lots of money so you can buy a sportscar
and fur for your girl [daughter]."

Guzzo would occasionally visit the Poulos home
where his confident manner, worldly ways and imposing
presence – his 1.8 metre frame carried almost 136 kg –

came to have a profound impact on the impressionable Micheline. Quite simply, he was the successful version of Poulos' hapless father. Guzzo told Micheline that her father was not a man because "a man always looks after his family," she recalled. "He [Guzzo] was to be my adviser. He said he could help me become someone and that I didn't have much chance of personal and financial success with my parents. I was looking for friendship, for someone who could love me. I was ashamed of where I lived, of myself, and of my family."

Within months of meeting Micheline, Guzzo began to spend nights at the Poulos residence, many of them in Micheline's twin bed. This wasn't an easy feat, considering his girth could easily occupy a kingsize bed. Soon, he was manoeuvering a brand new double bed into the home, explaining it was more comfortable for him and his new girlfriend. Amazingly, Poulos' parents didn't seem to care one way or the other if Guzzo slept over. Their silence, however, spoke volumes.

Oddly enough, no real passion took place behind the closed doors of Micheline Poulos' bedroom. Although she was under his spell, there was no lovemaking. Guzzo felt that fondling a woman and having intercourse with her was "dirty." Instead, Micheline was instructed to give Guzzo sexual relief by masturbating him to orgasm. He didn't touch her, and thus their relationship was quickly defined: Micheline Poulos would do the giving while Guzzo greedily took.

Guzzo eventually convinced his young girlfriend to move to Montreal, where, at first, she stayed with relatives. This arrangement lasted several months but ended when Poulos felt she was being harassed. Guzzo subsequently instructed her to live with his ailing widowed mother in Montreal. "My 'godfather' made me understand it was my duty to look after his mother," Micheline recalled.

Within a couple of years, Guzzo's mother's condition worsened and Micheline felt out of her depth caring for her. Some nights, Guzzo would sleep over in a separate bed, while Micheline slept with his mother. "One night his mother went to the kitchen and fell. Mr. Guzzo came to wake me up. He told me it was my fault, that I should have been looking after her. He said there was nothing I could do, I was too stupid to do anything for her." With that, Guzzo sent Micheline to the livingroom and ordered her to sit in a chair next to his mother, who was sleeping on a pull-out couch. "He told me if something happened to his mother, he would hold me responsible. I couldn't sleep because I was so afraid of something happening to me."

Guzzo's mother died within four years of Micheline moving in. Micheline then moved in with the "godfather," maintaining the same bedroom but separate beds. The arrangement was the same as it had been in St. Sauveur: when Guzzo felt like climaxing she was there to relieve him. Whatever needs she had were never acknowledged. By the mid-seventies, however, Micheline began to feel stymied by the relationship, which now included another woman, Olga Narepecka. Poulos wanted to go out with friends, meet young men, and enjoy the money she was now making as a bank teller. She wanted a life. She asked Guzzo if she could move out. If he let her, she promised to maintain their relationship on weekends. He agreed and she secured her own place. But it was Guzzo's name on the lease, Guzzo who managed her finances, Guzzo who told her what furniture to buy, what to wear and how to aspire in her career. "I'm going to do something, I'm going to make something of you," Guzzo would frequently tell Poulos. "If you follow me, you will be of worth, you will succeed in life."

In 1970 Frank Guzzo had met another woman who was eager to rebuild her life. Olga Narepecka, 39, was a pleasant, reserved divorcee, given to wearing pretty felt hats with feathers, a string of pearls around her neck, and feminine crepe and cotton dresses. Guzzo had been acquainted with her ex-husband.

Olga was concerned about how she would support herself after the demise of her marriage. True, she was "a trained secretary" but would that be enough? Guzzo stepped in and told her to forget about a meagre secretary's salary. "We'll open a boutique," he said.

However, "while there were many plans made, never was a boutique opened," she said. Despite this, Olga found herself increasingly dependent on the "god-father." Eventually, she came to live with him.

What attracted her to the man? "I think what impressed me most was the way he spoke. I found that he chose almost every word. Everything seemed to be so exact and that's what I was so impressed with." Occasionally, he would give her $100 to put in her wallet and instructed her to put cheques in the bank to cover their living expenses.

Although Olga had a son, Guzzo forbade her from seeing him. Instead, he would occassionally telephone her ex-husband to find out how the boy was doing. "I saw him [my son] about eight, nine years ago when Mr. Guzzo made an appointment to see him. Mr. Guzzo went out of the house to see him and then brought my son back to the house. That would be the only time I saw him."

Although Olga accepted what she felt was her lot in life, "I was always very nervous and always very fearful. There were always words or insinuations from a man," she said, "who could not tolerate a negative word." Still, she tried to please him. One day "he mentioned he had a taste for lemon pie so I became very eager and offered to bake one for him. He asked me what was involved. So I gave him the ingredients and said I would need a pie plate. He seemed to agree to everything but there was no pie plate and he asked me what it would cost. I told him it would be about $2. I was so eager to please him and he goes from his chair and came over and struck me across the face. It was much worse than a slap," she said crying. "Over the years, I would console myself with the thought that sometimes life is hard, sometimes life is good and I also feared him so it was unthinkable for me to try to get away so I just coped."

Although Poulos had moved out of the Cavendish Towers where Olga and Guzzo lived, she spent most of her free time with the "godfather" and Narepecka, who was now referred to as her "godmother." Despite the obvious complications of a love triangle, Guzzo managed to simplify even this relationship. Narepecka was his "companion," he said, and although she wasn't on equal footing with him, she was still a rung higher than Poulos, who was regarded as "the child." Interestingly, Guzzo told Olga he never loved Micheline. "He only functioned with his reasoning mind and never with emotions," Narepecka said. There was no rivalry between the pair because "Mr. Guzzo was always in control. He set the rules that there would be no animosity, no dissension."

Not surprisingly, Micheline was not altogether happy with this arrangement, and she struggled to build a life of her own. Guzzo would have none of it. He used his now-feeble Mob connections and threatened to spill acid in her face if she didn't obey him. She believed he had the clout to do just that, and she lived in mortal fear of his wrath.

He continued to control her finances, only letting her take out $100 at a time. When she would challenge him, he called her a slut. "If you leave me you won't succeed, you will be nothing, you fucking whore." Sometimes these emotional explosions gave way to violence, with Guzzo slapping Micheline Poulos so hard the imprints of his fingers would be left on her cheek. One time Poulos was slapped for bringing home spaghettini, instead of the thicker spaghetti noodle he had ordered.

Predictably, Poulos was unable to make any real friends and there was no one for her to confide in, except Guzzo. "She was forbidden to have a boyfriend. She

Mae Favell (right) receives words of support from friend Doris Horne outside the Kenora, Ont., courthouse October 1986. (Gerard Kwiatkowski/*Winnipeg Sun*)

Elouise Roads Wilson discusses her murder case with Vancouver journalist Larry Still. (Ralph Bower/*Vancouver Sun*)

The home in Vancouver's Shaughnessy district where Marion Colborn Hamilton was found strangled December 1975. (*Vancouver Sun*)

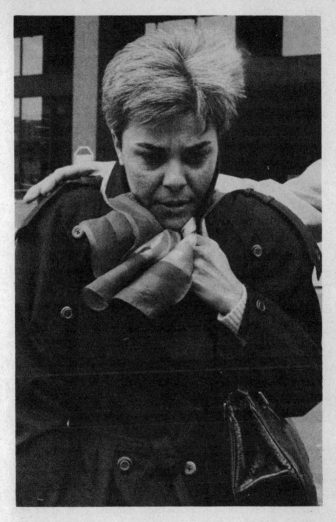

Micheline Poulos leaves a Montreal courtroom in May 1990 after being found guilty of killing the domineering mobster Frank Guzzo. (Pierre Coté/*Canapress*)

A relieved Cheryl Lynn Tutty (centre) and her lawyer Joel Pink meet with reporters in August 1986 after she received a suspended sentence for manslaughter in the death of her newborn baby. (*Canapress*)

Agathe Brochu (top left) orchestrated the bloody murder of her stingy common-law husband Wilf Gaudreault (top right) at their home in Kapuskasing, Ont.

Richard Boucher did the actual killing of Gaudreault and later hanged himself in jail.

Toronto cabbie Robert Pearson with his wife, Irene. Pearson's readiness to lend a helping hand to whoever asked brought him to an untimely and gruesome end in the spring of 1978. (Photo courtesy Irene Pearson)

Harriet Giesecke (top left) plotted the death of her estranged husband, Randall Giesecke (top right), in the fall of 1986.

Bruce Lynch was accused with Harriet Giesecke in the murder of her husband but was found not guilty. He later married Harriet.

Khristine Linklater killed her abusive husband with a
rifle blast in the summer of 1978. But thanks, in part, to
public support, counselling, and her religious faith, the
Yukon native was able to put the incident behind her and
obtain parole in 1982. (Frank Jones/*Toronto Star*)

could not have any significant relationship other than him," a psychologist would remark later. "She could have relationships at work but when she was home, she was to wait at her apartment for his phone call ... He kept her self-esteem low. He told her that she was nothing without him." Through passive reinforcement, Guzzo was able to convince Poulos that these difficult times were preparing her for her ultimate goal, namely "worthiness." It was somewhat akin to the Christian mode of thinking, wherein this life is one of suffering in preparation for a greater good – heaven. And Guzzo, according to the psychologist, was a "God who needed followers."

In the meantime, Micheline's co-workers had no idea what a twisted life their colleague was leading. She was competent at her job – in fact she had been promoted to assistant branch manager – was pleasant in conversation and frequently talked of her weekends away with her "godmother" and "godfather." To them, she seemed well-adjusted and most discreet about her private life. Hers appeared a most uneventful existence.

Early on the evening of January 5, 1990, members of the Côte St. Luc medical rescue department were dispatched to a one-bedroom apartment in the Cavendish Club Towers in west-end Montreal. An elderly man was reported to have suffered a cardiac arrest.

Zig-zagging through Montreal's narrow streets in a stationwagon were attendants Jonathan Lack and Ilan

Rose. They were volunteers for a first-response emergency measures department designed to provide care as quickly as possible in advance of regular ambulance service.

With the 23-year-old Rose at the wheel for his first time, the duo did well, arriving at Cavendish Club Towers within two minutes of being dispatched. At 7:30 they rang the buzzer for the address they'd been given, and a calm-sounding woman, speaking French, told them to "come on up." She pressed the entrance buzzer.

Opening the door to the apartment was a petite woman with cropped salt and pepper hair, her brown eyes sunk deep in a sallow face. A waft of cigarette smoke poured from the suite. Inside, ashtrays were stuffed with butts and the walls, once a cream colour, were now a mustard yellow from nicotine film. Lack, 25, asked where the patient was and the woman, Micheline Poulos, said he was in the bedroom but "you don't have to rush."

On the way to the bedroom he noticed a woman who appeared to be in her seventies sitting straight up in the living room, an afghan covering her legs. Her eyes were fixed on a black-and-white television blaring in the livingroom. The grey-haired woman seemed completely oblivious to Lack and made him feel uneasy.

Poulos led Lack to the bedroom. Gesturing with her hand, she showed him where the supposed cardiac-arrest sufferer was but refused to go into the room herself. On a bed was an emaciated man laying on his left side, his glassy eyes staring blankly at a wall. Lack immediately noticed a "head trauma." Two or three litres of blood had been absorbed by the mattress. Lack checked for a pulse but couldn't get one. Not immediately realizing the seriousness of the injury, he began to put an airway into the man's mouth to try to resuscitate him.

As he placed the black plastic tube into the man's mouth, he noticed a bloodied hole in the man's forehead, above the left eye. Wearing gloves, Lack lightly touched the area. The bone crumpled and flaked. A charred, black area surrounded the gash. "That's when I knew it was a gunshot wound." Clearly the man was dead.

Lack was frightened. "I started looking for a gun nearby, hoping it was a suicide but I couldn't find one." That made him even more nervous. A likely murderer, it seemed, was in their midst. He told Rose to radio for help in code so the two women wouldn't get excited. Lack yelled for Poulos but she didn't answer until the third call. Even then, she refused to go into the room. He met her at the bedroom doorway and asked her what had happened.

"I shot him," she replied flatly.

"You shot him?"

She nodded. Lack then asked her where the gun was and she pointed to a chair in the hall. Nestled there was a .38 calibre handgun, commonly referred to on the street as a "Saturday night special." Next to it was a box of bullets. An edgy Lack grabbed the gun, eager to get it into his possession. At this point, Poulos seemed to feel she owed some explanation. "He was very sick and he asked me to shoot him," she said.

"Was it cancer?" Lack inquired.

"Yes."

Poulos said she needed to sit down. Although calm at first, the 36-year-old now started to show signs of distress. Tears trickled down her cheek, and she began to smoke one cigarette after another. Lack got a glass of water from the kitchen and tried to calm her. Asked if the man's cancer was terminal, Poulos said she didn't know because he had refused to seek a doctor's opinion. Alternately wiping her nose with a tissue and sniffling, she confessed she had shot Frank Guzzo about 30 minutes before she telephoned for help. She killed him, she said, because he had been suffering with the dreaded disease for 18 months. She wanted to see him out of his suffering.

Lack felt he could bring his guard down and relax a little. It was finally starting to make sense. Looking around, he saw bandages and gauze, what looked like the aids of a sick patient. The victim, who appeared in his late sixties, had stubble for hair and he looked rather like a skeleton with skin. His temples were indented, his skin discoloured and yellowed. It seemed plausible that he was terminally ill.

Minutes later, ambulance attendants made it to the apartment and Lack told them what had happened. The police are going to be pissed off the gun was moved, they told him. Maybe he should put it back where he found it. Lack, still wearing his gloves, went into the bedroom and picked up the weapon from the top of the bureau. He walked to the hall chair and discovered Micheline Poulos sitting there. Evidence had been disrupted.

Officers from the Montreal Urban Community Police, the main force in the city, were next on the scene. The entire apartment was a haze of smoke. The elderly woman, Olga Narepecka, continued to sit in a trance-like state. Apparently in severe shock, she was taken to the hospital while officers took a statement from Micheline Poulos. There was no hesitation. She admitted to killing one Frank Guzzo, 56, by firing a full magazine of six bullets into the back of his head. On first inspection the death seemed a planned murder. The bedspread, for example, had been pulled off the twin bed where the dead man lay, in an apparent attempt at avoiding a nasty mess.

Meanwhile, officers went door-to-door in the highrise apartment building, looking for tenants who may have heard or seen something. What emerged was a disturbing portrait of a bizarre man: Guzzo, it seems, had not left his apartment, or even walked into the hallway, for seven years! As for Micheline and Olga, well, nobody really knew them. They were quiet tenants, polite.

Police felt they had a rather uncomplicated case on their hands. They had the killer, the victim, a star witness (Narepecka), a confession, a motive and the gun. A mercy killing undertaken by a woman who felt nothing but compassion for a man whose body was ravaged by cancer.

The gun had been purchased by Poulos years ago on the orders of Guzzo. Since Poulos was a bank teller, he felt she needed a gun if a hold-up turned ugly. After obtaining the firearm, she had taken shooting classes. She also owned a couple of rifles.

But when Poulos and Narepecka gave their confessions to Detective Sergeant Serge Côté, he heard a story unlike anything he had heard in his 24 years on the force.

Poulos and Narepecka spoke of being slaves to the whims
of Guzzo – a slavery whose shackles were removed only
with his death.

Catering to the headstrong, cranky Guzzo had proved
especially onerous to Narepecka. Her once supple skin
had become leathery in texture, her once classy wardrobe
was now a collection of dowdy smocks and clunky shoes.
Exhaustion seemed to weigh her every move. "In my
opinion she seemed to be a zombie," Côté observed.
"She was super-polite, wouldn't hurt a fly and looked like
a slave."

Matters got worse when Guzzo became seriously ill.
He was convinced he was dying of cancer but refused to
be diagnosed by a doctor because he had no confidence in
the medical profession. By 1988, gangrenous infections
could be seen on his feet, blisters formed on his toes. His
legs ached constantly. He became impotent. His weight
dropped by almost two hundred pounds. Day in, day
out, Narepecka rinsed the yellowish-green poison that
seeped from his feet, and fed him the only painkiller he
trusted, aspirin.

Narepecka was assisted on weekends and most eve-
nings by Poulos, who continued to pay rent on her own
apartment. Narepecka and Guzzo would sleep on separate twin beds. Poulos would stay in the same bedroom,
too, sleeping on thin cushions scattered on the floor. By
December of 1989, an exhausted Narepecka said she
needed more help. At Guzzo's urging, Poulos agreed to
quit her bank job and move into the one-bedroom suite
to provide Guzzo with round-the-clock care.

The cramped apartment became a kind of war zone.

Guzzo constantly harangued his two attendants and forbade them to speak to each other unless he permitted it. They were not allowed to speak with him unless he spoke first. He insisted Poulos call him the "godfather" whenever she addressed him.

To all appearances, Poulos was a compliant, passive victim. But she was not entirely without a mind of her own. Guzzo, she thought, might be wrong about his illness. Maybe it wasn't cancer. Without his permission, she went to the public library to consult medical dictionaries and determine if cancer could cause circulation problems and foot sores. She discovered that Guzzo most likely was suffering from untreated diabetes. However, when she tried to tell him, he pooh-poohed her diagnosis. After all, he was God in the apartment and God knows everything.

On the evening of January 4, 1990, Guzzo called Micheline Poulos into the bedroom. "If I asked you to kill me, would you do it?" he asked. Poulos made no reply.

"I know that I am sick," Guzzo went on. "If I wanted to die, would you do it?" Poulos this time nodded in agreement but she didn't think Guzzo was talking about anything that would happen in the near future.

However, the next day he informed both women that he was too tired to continue living and really did want to die. The morose Guzzo told Narepecka that Poulos would do the actual deed. She would fire six bullets into his brain, then wait at least a half-hour before calling the police. "I don't want to survive," he said. "I don't want any doctor to have a chance of reviving me."

Moreover, he observed, since Olga wasn't feeling too

well either, perhaps Micheline could kill Narepecka as
well. Of course, perpetrating two murders would inevit-
ably result in a lengthy jail sentence for Poulos. If, that is,
she were to remain alive. Perhaps, Guzzo ruminated, it
might be best if Micheline took her own life after
despatching him and Narepecka.

A stunned Narepecka doddered into the living room
and sat down. Poulos called a taxi and went to her apartment to pick up her handgun and ammunition. She
stashed the weapon and bullets into a paper bag and
made her way back to Guzzo's apartment. Deep down,
Poulos confessed later, she hoped someone, somewhere,
somehow would step in to prevent her from killing the
"godfather." Alas, no one did.

Back at the apartment, she stood over Guzzo's bed and
said a few words to the man who had ruled her life for the
past 18 years. Guzzo's back was to her. In rapid succes-
sion, she fired one shot after another until the only sound
in the bedroom was the clicking of the gun hammer. All
of the bullets had hit Guzzo's head, some of them going
clear through his skull and scattering throughout the
bedroom. Blood splattered the room. The stench of the
gun smoke was unlike anything she had ever smelled
before, it was nauseating. But, finally, the years of pain
and suffering seemed to be over. Guzzo was dead.

Poulos walked into the living room. Narepecka was
still sitting there, seemingly unnerved. She had heard the
shots and knew what had happened. In a rare moment,
the pair broke the Guzzo-imposed silence: they cried.
Then they smoked cigarette after cigarette until a

half-hour passed. Poulos walked over to the telephone and dialed 911. She identified herself and calmly stated that a very close friend was dead. When the dispatcher asked her what was wrong, she replied, "it's very difficult for me to talk." With that, the death was called in as a cardiac arrest.

Micheline Poulos was booked at the homicide office on Beausecours Street in Old Montreal on a charge of first-degree murder and taken to a holding cell. Narepecka wasn't charged because police felt she had nothing to do with it. "She had no way of knowing what was going to happen until the last minute," said Sergeant Côté.

Legal Aid assigned Robert Sachitelle, 52, as Poulos' counsel. He had been a lawyer for almost 26 years and enjoyed a reputation as a defender of the downtrodden and politically active.

Sachitelle met Poulos in an interview room. She was calm at first. Sitting there, thick, black eyebrows curving over swollen eyes, Poulos explained that Guzzo had asked her to kill him. Sachitelle realized his client hadn't really grasped the fact that she was charged with premeditated murder.

"Suddenly, when I explained what a murder was, she started to cry," he would later recall. "I never wanted to kill him," she explained. "I still want him right there beside me."

First-degree murder carried a heavy sentence, Sachitelle knew. Mandatory life imprisonment, in fact, without eligibility for parole for 25 years. But maybe, just maybe, it wouldn't have to end that way, he thought.

The trial of Micheline Poulos opened May 7, 1990 in Montreal with a Québec Superior Court jury of seven men and five women before Crown prosecutor André Vincent, defence lawyer Robert Sachitelle and Mr. Justice Fraser Martin.

Sachitelle planned to base his defence on Micheline's lack of personal will power at the time of Frank Guzzo's death. According to Luc Granger, Director of Psychology at the University of Montreal, as well as a criminologist and two psychiatrists, Micheline Poulos was suffering from "dependent personality syndrome," a passive-aggressive condition similar to that experienced by women who endure 30-year marriages with alcoholic husbands.

"It didn't surprise me she had been with him 18 years, she could have stayed longer," Granger later said in an interview. Poulos was in a submissive state, unable to refuse Guzzo's order to kill because of it. Her self as an autonomous entity could not and did not exist without Guzzo. Minus the "godfather," she was nothing. With him, she was on the path to worthiness. No matter how difficult, how painful or disturbing it could be, it would all be worth it in the end when her final accomplishment was realized.

Of course, who knows if in the back of Poulos' mind, she secretly wished Guzzo dead. There must have been times when she fantasized about being free. His evil temper, his razor-sharp tongue, his insults were, at times, provocative. With a blast from a gun, she could have the last word.

The Crown's André Vincent attacked the dependent personality defence. If she was so much under Guzzo's spell, he asked, why did she refuse his wish for a murder-suicide? If Poulos was as out of control as the defence experts agreed, what stopped her from firing a bullet into Narepecka, then herself?

Technically speaking, this was, Vincent suggested, a cut-and-dried case of first-degree murder. In a post-trial interview, he acknowledged the death was a mercy killing – but that it should not go unpunished. "I do think she killed him out of compassion," he said later. "My job is to present the evidence and put it before the jury." Indeed, she planned the assassination, went to her home, picked up the gun, ammunition, loaded it, neatly took off the bedspread and then killed him. It was deliberate, thought out. No one could disagree with that.

Another point made during the trial was Poulos' admission that she probably would have refused killing the "godfather" had he not been terminally ill. At what point was Poulos completely under Guzzo's control? When he was completely incapacitated?

Interestingly, the court was told that, in fact, Guzzo was hardly completely incapacitated at the time of his death, nor did he have terminal cancer. The autopsy revealed that the mobster was suffering from generalized arteriosclerosis, more commonly known as hardening of

the arteries. True, Guzzo did have a scar on the left vent-
ricle of his heart and there were signs of gangrene on his
feet but "according to the coroner, he wasn't dying of
anything," a police officer said. "He would have lived
quite a few years."

Countering Vincent, Sachitelle argued that the reason
Poulos hadn't killed Narepecka or herself was because
Guzzo had only *suggested* that scenario. Had he actually
ordered her to carry it out, who knows, perhaps she
would have.

As the trial progressed, a sobbing Micheline gradually
became more self-conscious, more aware of the intolera-
ble life she had led. The trial, in effect, became a kind of
therapy. "She realized by listening to what the psychiatrists said, that something was wrong," Sachitelle said
later. "I think now, after hearing her own background,
she realizes it was not the relationship she thought it was.
It was not normal to be submissive that way."

By the end of the one-week trial, the jury seemed to
sway to Poulos' side. But while they were moved by her
struggles, they were in a difficult position. In his charge
to the jury, Justice Martin warned that consent on the
part of the victim cannot be used to justify any killing,
morally or legally. Admittedly, Poulos suffered from low
self-esteem, aggravated by a climate of fear in the Guzzo
home but none of the specialists had testified that the
woman suffered from a quantifiable mental handicap.
Even Sachitelle acknowledged that working up a defence
for Poulos had been difficult. "You couldn't say [the mur-
der] was self-defence, or that she was mentally ill …

Basically we tried to present the background, that Poulos was not in possession of her own will so therefore her act was actually unconscious."

On Friday, May 11, 1990, and after 17 hours of difficult deliberations, Micheline Poulos was found guilty of the lesser charge of manslaughter. One week later she was sentenced to three years imprisonment. She is currently serving her time in a Montreal prison. Narepecka is living a quiet life in the same city.

SEVEN

Keeping it in the Family

Phillip Wilson tucked his wife's cousin, Marion Colborn Hamilton, into her bed in the first-floor study. The bed was, in fact, a cot and an uncomfortable one at that. It also didn't "fit" with the ornate antique furniture and art that were crammed into the ivy-covered Vancouver mansion that Hamilton owned. Hamilton herself didn't seem to fit in there, either. She was an eccentric lady who rebelled against the family who cared for her. Sometimes, Phillip and his wife, Elouise Roads Wilson, would have to tie the 69-year-old Hamilton to her wheelchair for a moment of peace.

Fortunately, December 1, 1975, was different. Hamilton was cooperative and Phillip Wilson was happy there wasn't the usual fuss at bed-time. After he tucked Hamilton in with a hot-water bottle, he kissed her goodnight. He then left the home with the stucco exterior at 1491 Nanton shortly after 7 p.m. to catch the ferry to Victoria which would take him close to his home in Crofton. Elouise Wilson remained with Hamilton.

Profoundly senile, Hamilton couldn't look after herself. Born August 12, 1906 to a wealthy Irish family, she lived in Ottawa for many years before moving to Vancouver with her husband, an army officer. He later died of cancer.

The only person seemingly more eccentric than Marion Hamilton was Elouise Roads Wilson, 46. She had black straight hair, parted in the middle. Her rouge was a strong red and heavily applied in streaks to her cheeks. Her lips were painted unevenly with a creamy red geranium lipstick. She was a short, stocky woman with the gait of an old, fat dog. It was hard to believe that she came from a family of British Columbia notables. Her grandfather was Eli Harrison, one of the province's pioneer jurists. Two uncles, both lawyers, had gone on to be mayors of Victoria and Nanaimo, respectively. Elouise herself was a lawyer, having graduated from the University of British Columbia in 1957 – a time when female barristers were a decided rarity.

Despite Elouise's rather grotesque appearance, outsiders thought it nice that the Wilsons took care of Hamilton. Except for one other cousin, Olga Young, the Wilsons were Hamilton's last hope. Elouise decided to take time off from her law practise to care for her ailing cousin until she found something better to do with her.

On December 2, 1975 Elouise Wilson awoke at 8:30 a.m.

and, on entering the first-floor study, noticed that Hamilton was lying not in her cot but in a slightly curled position on the floor. She called the ambulance attendants right away. When they arrived, they were directed to the study by Elouise, who was busy sweeping the kitchen floor.

A sombre attendant returned with the news. "I'm afraid she's dead," he said. Wilson stopped, looked at him and said, "Oh, that's too bad," and continued her household chores.

Not surprisingly, the attendant was struck by Wilson's odd behaviour. Her apparent indifference seemed equally matched by a pleasant demeanour. Although it seemed a routine sudden death, the police would have to be summoned before the body could be removed, he explained. Wilson nodded in agreement and went about her cleaning.

In the meantime, the ambulance attendants made notes. Moist blood from Hamilton's nose, mouth, and ears had flowed and dried in an upward position. Streaks of blood zig-zagged across her face from ear to ear. The face itself was puckered, the prominent nose filled with caked-on blood, her arms thin and shrivelled. Urine and blood were on the carpet and an upended bed pan lay to the east of the body. Across the room was the small cot with a hot-water bottle on it. The cot wasn't made. Hamilton herself was wearing a green suit jacket over a brown sweater, and white pants with white stockings, as well as a light blue housecoat, wet with urine.

Uniformed officers arrived at the manor and took

pictures of Hamilton. Street cops don't necessarily take photographs of sudden deaths – this is usually left to identification officers. However, since Vancouver had been plagued by a rash of sudden deaths and break-ins, officers were being given cameras to keep in their cars for the sake of efficiency. As police finished up, two more ambulance attendants arrived around 9:30 to whisk the body away. But first they removed a gold necklace that was lodged in the crease of Hamilton's neck and handed it to police. Then she was transported to Vancouver General Hospital where, at 10:20, she was formally pronounced dead.

Initially, Marion Hamilton's sudden death was filed as "a collapse." But as the hours passed in the cold of the morgue, a distinct, reddish-purple line emerged around the woman's neck. Later, an autopsy would conclude that the death was caused by asphyxiation by ligature. The ligature mark was almost completely around the neck's circumference, forming a V in an upward line at the back. According to the autopsy, this mark could have resulted from a hanging or accidental suicide. Indeed, because the blood on the victim's face appeared to run upwards, it was likely Hamilton had been turned over just before death. Bruising and hemorrhaging were noted inside the upper lip, as well as inside the left upper eye lid and inside right upper eye lid. There were bruises, too, in back of the upper right forearm, below the left elbow, on the left calf and to the third and fourth knuckle.

Strange deaths were not uncommon at 1491 Nanton. Just eight months earlier, on March 18, 1975, neighbours complained of a horrendous smell emanating from the home. They thought it was rotting garbage. In fact, it was Hamilton's mother, Eunice Coote, 89, who, it turned out, had been dead – and undiscovered – for four to six weeks. Her decomposing body was found covered in flies. A poster depicting the signs of the zodiac lay on her chest. Marion Hamilton, who was living in the house, said she didn't even notice her mother was dead. No autopsy was ordered on Coote because police and the coroner surmised she expired from natural causes.

After this traumatic event, Marion Hamilton's behaviour grew increasingly bizarre. She would buy a half-dozen cans of cat food each day for several weeks until the pantry at 1491 Nanton was stocked with hundreds of tins. Marion Hamilton, it should be noted, had no cat. Late at night, she would go for solitary walks. When she returned, she would have to ask her neighbours for help because she had locked herself out.

Superficially at least, 1491 Nanton seemed an unlikely setting for a homicide. The house was located in Shaughnessy, and Shaughnessy is to Vancouver what Westmount is to Montreal and Rosedale is to Toronto. The area is filled with huge, rambling mansions. There are stucco, Tudor-style homes mixed with those with the California influence of huge windows and pastel colours. In the alleyways and streets are late-model Mercedes Benz, Porsches and BMWs. For the most part, residents are immaculately-dressed, high-powered, and discreet in their behaviour.

On the night of December 2 when detectives Ken

Hale and Roy Chapman from the major crime unit of Vancouver police knocked on the door of 1491 Nanton, they were met by a woman whose poorly applied cheap makeup and scruffy clothing made her look more like a housekeeper than a wealthy lawyer. It was, however, Elouise Wilson.

The detectives were awed by the house. Piled in a mountainous heap on the dining room table was every form of houseware imaginable – plates, cutlery, teapots. Coming upon it thieves would have likened it to Christmas or early retirement. Art Nouveau bronze statues and framed Victorian art that would fetch thousands of dollars gave the interior a museum-like atmosphere. The doors of the home had ornate leaded crystal knobs. And the hardwood parquet floors were immaculately finished.

Hale informed Wilson that he and Chapman would be collecting evidence such as fingerprints and anything else they deemed relevant. For her part, Wilson seemed completely uninterested in the proceedings and didn't ask a single question. She sat in the front room of the home watching television, her eyes never straying as the detectives moved about the house.

Inspecting the study, Hale thought it peculiar that for such a well-appointed house, Marion Hamilton had slept in a flimsy cot tucked away in a corner. Next to the cot was an overstuffed leather chair with wood trim. Peering behind the chair, he noticed a long piece of twine with a blue piece of plastic woven into it, later found to be polypropylene cord. Was this the string, he wondered, that stopped the life of Marion Colborn Hamilton? He reached over, grabbed it, and later handed it to Vancouver City Analyst's Laboratory, along with a white pillow case with black marks found on the bed.

Hale wondered if anyone might have broken into the house. He noticed that while there had been a light snowfall recently, no footprints were found near any of the outside windows – a sign that a burglary was unlikely. He checked the window sills for jimmy marks. Again, nothing.

After the inspection, Chapman asked Elouise Wilson to recount what had happened. She told him that at about 7 p.m. on December 1, she and her husband, Phillip Wilson, had put Hamilton into bed with a hot-water bottle. Marion was quiet as they tucked her in, and they left the night light on. Phillip then left at 7:10 p.m. to catch the 9 o'clock ferry to Victoria from Horseshoe Bay.

The following morning, Elouise Wilson said she went to Hamilton's room, opened the door and saw her cousin unconscious on the floor, wearing the same clothes they had put her to sleep in. Wilson said she pushed the door to get in but "hardly moved the body." She couldn't remember if her ailing cousin was wearing a necklace or not. The thick, gold chain had been a present from Wilson, who gave it to Hamilton to hang her house key from. Neither Hale nor Chapman wished to jump to any conclusions but later, after questioning of Wilson, Hale turned to his partner and said: "I think this is our person right here."

Wilson was both a most unlikely and likely suspect.

Unlikely because she was a wealthy lawyer who had her own country practice in the small village of Crofton, northeast of Duncan, on Vancouver Island. Likely because she was the residual beneficiary of Eunice Coote's estate which had been left first to Hamilton.

Born September 28, 1929 in Crofton, Elouise Wilson was a woman of privilege but despite her pedigree she seemed best known for her tasteless wardrobe. Clerks in the district business office of North Cowichen remembered her in the sixties for her floppy, wide-brimmed hats and mismatched dark polyester outfits. A distinct smell of body odour followed her. Her visits to the office were strictly business at first, usually applying to obtain tax certificates. But then she spotted Phillip Wilson, a senior clerk in the land titles office. A brief courtship ensued, followed by marriage.

Phillip Wilson was also a suspect in the Hamilton death, but not a major one, Hale would say years later in an interview. Although he claimed to have taken a ferry to Vancouver the night of December 1, there was no way to substantiate it. But, as Hale said, "I don't think he'd hurt his gums to brush his teeth." Wilson possessed a weak, quiet nature, odd looks, and suffered from a speech impediment. Life with the domineering Elouise consisted of walks, card-playing with friends, and working hard. Some say he married well: Elouise owned at least four homes on Vancouver Island.

Marion Hamilton's death went to a coroner's jury. After hearing medical evidence indicating she had died of asphyxia from a ligature, they concluded, on

December 22, 1975, that her death was the result of homicide. This murder didn't leave police with too many suspects. Not only was Elouise Wilson in the house when Marion Hamilton died (opportunity), she also was the main beneficiary (motive) in the deceased woman's will. It would add up to about $250,000, including house and contents.

While all the evidence against Elouise Wilson was admittedly circumstantial, it was damaging in its breadth and detail. Police, for instance, had located a letter addressed to Royal Trust, on letterhead from Wilson's law practice, dated October 10, 1975. It read:

> Re: Marion Hamilton
>   So far, no one has been asked to act for my aunt, Eunice B. Coote's estate.
>   Naturally the least expensive way to do this would be considered so that the beautiful home, the antiques and the funds are preserved and not sold, and the home not abused by renting (renters have no consideration for good properties).
>   I would appreciate a statement from you as to your charges in estate matters. Other companies, etc. will also be contacted for a comparison of charges.
>   In this day of escalating costs and general depression of business, the only sensible thing is to preserve properties and not sell.
>   I am seeing the Veteran's affairs re Mrs. Hamilton's service in the 1939–45 War in Red Cross ambulance and nursing and he has asked me to see him again in two weeks'

time. He is very encouraging. I will let you know after my next meeting.

A postscript read:

We still have not received a list of assets, liabilities and legal and other costs in the Hamilton estate.

To police, this was incriminating. Elouise seemed determinied to get her cousin out of 1491 Nanton and into a "free" Veteran's hospital, using Hamilton's Red Cross service as a pretext. Elouise would keep the house as a sort of nest egg.

On January 16, 1976, two detectives interviewed Elouise Wilson at the Victoria police station.

Detective: I want to go back to the night that you put Marion to bed. I understand Phillip had a conversation with Mrs. Young, he mentioned that Marion had wanted to go downtown that night?

Elouise: Yes, but we would not let her, all kinds of bad things could happen to her.

Detective: I believe she called you a 'crazy old bat?'

Elouise: Yes, she called everyone that, even the nurse.

Detective: I believe there was a tiff, she wanted some money and was determined to go?

Elouise: There was a tiff, she might have asked Phillip for some money. She was always determined, strong-minded.

On January 17, Elouise Wilson was charged with non-capital murder. She was stunned. At the time of her arrest, she rambled on, seemingly utterly amazed. "Why did you do that? You know I didn't do that. When did you get that warrant? Oh, today. Why didn't you have it yesterday? Were you going to do this [all] along, or were you going to charge me with a lesser thing? Who made you charge me with this? Why did you do it? I want to get out."

Wilson hired Robert Gardner, a young, bright Vancouver criminal lawyer known for his aggressive defences. Gardner planned to show there was a strong possibility that Marion Hamilton's death had been a suicide, not murder. To bolster his position, he planned to call a criminologist from Burnaby's Simon Fraser University, a Calgary forensic pathologist, and another pathologist from San Francisco.

However, three weeks before the start of the trial and just after the preliminary hearing, Wilson decided to not retain Gardner's services, saying she was not prepared to pay the high cost of his defence which, at $100 an hour plus expenses for expert witnesses, would have resulted in a hefty tab. When Gardner refused to take the trial unless he could call that defence, Wilson hired the veteran James Sutherland, a defence lawyer with the magnificent record of never seeing any of his clients convicted of murder. This was quite a feat, considering that he had practised in the days when a conviction often meant death by hanging. In his first two years of practice alone, he handled thirteen murder trials. Now in this early sixties, Sutherland had done and seen just about everything in criminal law.

When Wilson walked into the Vancouver offices of Sutherland and Sutherland, across the street from the courthouse, passersby couldn't help but stare. Wilson was a walking fashion disaster wearing a wide-brimmed, crumpled white hat and looking more upscale bag lady than lawyer. After talking with Wilson and looking at the evidence, Sutherland knew he was in for a tough haul. "It sounded pretty bad," he would recall later in an interview in Vancouver. "She was the only one in the house and her husband had gone back on the late ferry. It was very hard to think up a defence." Wilson also didn't seem to realize the significance of being charged with murder. "It was like somebody had accused a Sunday school teacher of smoking in public. She didn't put murder in a bad category."

Wilson remained calm and seemingly unworried as the trial began in June 1977 before a 10-member jury. People packed into the Supreme Court of British Columbia building, now the Vancouver Art Gallery, to get a peek of the accused murderer. The tale of how Marion Hamilton met her end seemed to promise the drama of an Agatha Christie mystery novel. Wilson, of course, pleaded not guilty.

Despite this protestation, Crown prosecutor John Hall thought the case a "pretty clearly proven" one. "The only person who had the opportunity and motive was her. It was an estate of some substance and Wilson was the residuary beneficiary of the deceased."

Throughout her trial Elouise remained undaunted by the attention she was attracting. It wasn't every day a lawyer is charged with murder. At times Wilson was stoic as the evidence was presented. Other times she furiously wrote notes in a loose-leaf binder as testimony piled against her. Oddly, she passed none of these notes to her lawyer. Reflecting on her trial today, Elouise likened the proceedings to "a kangaroo court." Standing by her through it all were her husband and father.

Unlike Gardner, Sutherland saw little merit in the suicide theory. For it to be possible, Marion would somehow have had to pull the cord in an upwards motion to the back of her neck and then tightly twist the rope until she strangled herself to death. After that, she would have had to grab the cord and throw it away. As well, given her degree of senility, it would be difficult if not impossible, he thought, to form the desire to die. Calling other experts, to him, seemed a needless expense and a futile exercise. Besides, Wilson simply didn't want it. As a result, Sutherland's defence consisted primarily of attacking the evidence and trying to raise reasonable doubt. He did this by suggesting that Phillip Wilson had as good a motive as his wife did in wanting the old woman dead. It was a stratagem Phillip Wilson agreed to, Sutherland said.

The strongest evidence against Elouise came from Olga Young, Marion Hamilton's other cousin. Several months before Eunice Coote's death, Hamilton told

Young, a woman in her late thirties, exactly what she wanted: for Young and her husband Cy to do the financing. Young declined because neither she nor her husband apparently wanted that burden. After Coote's death, Young contacted a doctor to see what she could do for Hamilton. The doctor urged Young to have Marion get a medical check-up and employ a full-time housekeeper and nurse. Hamilton refused. Realizing Hamilton could no longer care for herself, Young hired a lawyer to have her estate managed by a trust company, another move Hamilton did not appreciate.

When Young told her cousin, Elouise Wilson, of the arrangement she had made with the trust company, she was met with fierce opposition. Wilson told Young that all trust companies were crooked. Despite this difference of opinion, Young managed to have Royal Trust appointed to handle Hamilton's estate, which also included the almost $8,000 the old woman earned yearly from annuities.

In preparing the paperwork, Royal Trust officials informed Young that Hamilton would need a guardian. Since Young wasn't keen, she asked Wilson if she would be interested. It was an attractive if daunting offer and Wilson agreed, with one stipulation: that Young be her co-guardian. Wilson explained that Hamilton was "unfriendly" toward her and would not allow her into the house unless Young was there. Still, Wilson said she thought Hamilton's resentment might subside over time.

The animosity had always been there. It had surfaced again in March of 1975 when Elouise and her father decided to stay in their car for the duration of Eunice Coote's funeral service. Marion Hamilton was furious at this seeming disrespect and referred to Elouise Wilson as "that dreadful woman." Of course, Elouise's reluctance to attend the service might have had something to do with Hamilton's obvious disdain for her. To this day no one in the family can quite figure out the origins of the animosity.

Eventually, Young grudgingly agreed to be co-guardian, even though she wanted nothing to do with the finances, other than "setting them up." She vowed to remove herself once Hamilton adjusted to Wilson. Young told Wilson that eventually Hamilton would have to be placed in a private hospital. Failing that, a nursing home or a full-time housekeeper would be required. If none of these approaches worked, then they should consider sending her to a chronic care hospital.

Wilson, however, rejected all these ideas, citing the expense as too much for Hamilton to bear. Young called up the trust company. An official there told her that Hamilton could afford a private hospital and if the house were sold, she could more than afford it, using just the interest on the sale price alone. Wilson, however, accused the trust company of plotting to cut up the money for themselves, claiming Hamilton would end up a pauper if she went to a private hospital.

Young immediately realized that Wilson's viewpoint was "unreal" but her desire to avoid a quarrel overrode her need to press for what was right. She did mention that Hamilton on the day of her mother's funeral had asked to be moved into an apartment. Wilson, however, snorted that apartments were "low class"; and Marion Hamilton was a "high class" lady.

Throughout the spring and summer of 1975, Elouise Wilson spent many weekends at the Shaughnessy home, taking care of Hamilton, who had to make the best of it by herself during the week. When it came time for Wilson to return to Vancouver Island to more fully resume her practice, Young told her they would either have to place Hamilton in a hospital or get a housekeeper and a home nurse. Wilson rejected confining Hamilton in a hospital but said if she could find "cheap oriental help," then this person could care for her cousin at home.

Young decided to get ammunition to fight Wilson's recalcitrance. She talked with Hamilton's doctor, a psychiatrist, and trust company advisors, all of whom said placing Marion Hamilton in a private hospital would be the best alternative.

At the end of July, Young received a call one afternoon from Wilson who told her that their cousin had arrived home from shopping with a black eye. "I've heard quite enough of how Marion is no longer coping," Young told her. "Now it's beginning to look as though the poor woman's life is in danger." She told Wilson that she was rushing right over and she should bar Hamilton from trying to leave the house in the meantime.

When Young arrived, she found Wilson standing guard over the front door and a frenzied Hamilton banging away trying to get out. The pair managed to calm the poor, sick woman until a doctor and ambulance came to take her to a psychiatric ward. She was later transferred to the Shaughnessy Hospital but doctors told Young that her cousin would have to be removed because they could not accommodate Hamilton as a chronic care patient. Wilson proceeded to stall the hospital, saying she would remove her cousin but she did anything but. It wasn't until mid-November when the hospital began to charge her $26 a day – what Wilson termed a "dreadful expense" – that she finally removed Marion Hamilton.

At the end of October, Wilson offered to close down her law office and move into 1491 Nanton herself. Young agreed, provided the following conditions were met: the doctor agreed; the home was outfitted for semi-invalid care; and a nurse be there most of the time. Wilson relented, adding that if Hamilton showed even the slightest unease about the situation, she would immediately place her in a private hospital. In fact, she already had one picked out, a choice Hamilton had already agreed to.

On November 15 Wilson telephoned Young to say she and Hamilton had arrived at 1491 Nanton safe and sound. Young seemed pleased and said she would be over in a few days for a visit and to help arrange nursing care. Young called the home during the week but there was no answer.

At first, Young thought Wilson might have taken Hamilton out for a walk but it became apparent early on that either no one was there or the line was disconnected. She was about to call the operator to check the line when she received a call from Phillip Wilson. He told Young he thought she should know that Hamilton was in Victoria and had been there, in fact, since being released from hospital. Sounding nervous and upset, Phillip said his wife had tried to get her ailing father and mother to care for Hamilton in their home. When those plans failed, she had temporarily relocated Hamilton to her Victoria home but it was too cramped.

An astounded Young asked where Hamilton was now. Phillip said his wife had spent the better part of the day trying to get a friend to care for her cousin.

Young didn't mince words. She angrily told him she was upset and demanded to know when Hamilton would be returned to Vancouver. She told Wilson to get in touch with his wife immediately and have her phone. Young had had enough. She now thought Wilson was unfit to be Hamilton's guardian and immediately began to take steps to have her removed. A call was made to the trust company, another to a lawyer.

On November 24, Wilson finally called Young and told her that the voyage to Vancouver Island had been "purely a pleasure trip" because Hamilton had become unmanageable at the Shaughnessy home and claimed she didn't want to stay there.

Distraught, Young accused Wilson of dragging a "poor, sick old lady" all over the country and ordered her to bring the woman back to Vancouver. She had decided that a private hospital was the best place for Hamilton and she was making plans to place her in one. Wilson was adamantly against it and said the home must never be sold. She did concede, however, that Hamilton would need to be in a hospital full-time at some point, just not now.

On Sunday, November 30, Young told Wilson that she would be coming over the next day. "When I come I want to see how you are feeding her and what kind of bed she has." On December 1, Young spent the better part of the day making arrangements for a physician to regularly examine Hamilton. She also obtained the names and telephone numbers of three companies specializing in nursing care. That afternoon, she called Wilson and told her of the plans she had made. Wilson told Young she didn't want a nurse in the home because they might steal some of the antiques. Wilson reiterated one last time that the house was not to be sold and the estate was to remain untouched. That was the end of it.

On the morning of December 2, Elouise Wilson telephoned Olga Young shortly after 8:30 with some bad news.

"Nanny's dead," Wilson said. "She's cold."

"Good God, no! Call Vancouver General and tell them to send a doctor and do it quickly!"

When ambulance attendants arrived, however, they found Marion Hamilton to be quite warm – an indication that her death had not occurred all that long ago.

Olga Young's story seemed most damaging. But James Sutherland vigorously argued that his client was merely caught in a "web of circumstantial evidence." He said the motive and opportunity were the same for her husband,

Phillip. Although he was supposed to be on his way back to Victoria, the defence lawyer said the Crown had presented no evidence to show he reached his destination. "His motive might have been as strong as hers," he said. A second scenario may have involved a burglary that, when bungled, turned into murder. Sutherland repeatedly stressed to the jury that it need only find a reasonable doubt in the Crown's case to acquit his client. "There's not one iota of evidence here other than motive and opportunity that points to the guilt of the accused," he said, "and Mrs. Wilson cannot be convicted merely because of motive and opportunity."

In his closing address, Hall, who years later would successfully handle the prosecution of serial killer Clifford Olson, told the jury that the evidence against Wilson ran like a river – all one way. He questioned Wilson's motives for leaving her law practice to care for a woman she hadn't even been on speaking terms with. "Was she doing it for love, or money?" he asked the jury.

He argued there was "an astounding lack of evidence" to suggest that the home was burgled and Marion was killed during it. "He's a curious burglar, because he doesn't leave much trace of himself." For that theory to be credible, the intruder would have had to break into the occupied living room of the house, strangle Hamilton, carefully hide in the room the length of nylon cord alleged to be the murder weapon, fail to steal anything, and then sneak out of the house without leaving a trace.

After deliberating for two hours and 15 minutes, the jury returned on July 2, 1977 with a guilty verdict of second-degree murder against Elouise Roads Wilson. Asked by Justice Craig F. Munroe if she had anything to say before sentencing was passed, Wilson asked for a moment to consult with her lawyer. "I have been advised by legal counsel not to say anything," she said.

The judge then sentenced her to the mandatory life imprisonment. Eight months later, on March 31, 1978, Wilson would be disbarred by the Law Society of British Columbia by "reason of her being convicted of an indictable offence."

Wilson was floored by the verdict. She had no idea that she would be convicted. "I was in a complete state of shock as I was driven to Oakalla (prison). How could they convict me?" she said in an interview with the *Vancouver Sun*'s Larry Still. "The evidence was so vague. There wasn't a shred to link me with Marion's death. I could never do such a thing. It is against my nature." She cited her long-time membership in the Pro Life Society as an example of how she was incapable of taking life in any form. "I had no idea they would charge me with such an absurd thing. I had absolutely nothing to do with my cousin's death. I couldn't do such a thing. I couldn't take the life of an animal, let alone a person." Wilson said she was so confident before her trial's start that the Crown's circumstantial case would be rejected that she instructed Sutherland not to call any evidence for the defence.

During the interview, she told Still that she was shocked by the violent behaviour and language of the inmates at the remand centre, and admitted she had difficulty adjusting to the culture. "You get picked on by the heavies if you can't talk about dope and prostitution and turning tricks. I had no idea women could be so violent." She managed to survive the grim environment by studying Latin "so that I couldn't hear the terrible shrieks and the fights that went on all around me."

Lawyer Allan McEachern, who was later appointed Chief Justice of the B.C. Supreme Court, handled her first appeal, which was unsuccessful. When avenues of appeal seemed exhausted, the convicted murderer turned to the person she had gone to in the first place for help – Robert Gardner.

Gardner still believed his suicide theory had credibility and he had the media smarts to get it into the newspapers and on television and radio. The *Vancouver Sun,* for one, ran a front page story in 1978, stating that he had new evidence to suggest that Marion Hamilton may have killed herself. "Suicide theory cited in 'murder' – Lawyer tries to reopen bizarre murder case," it read. Gardner's theory, which was supported by the opinions of two forensic pathologists and a criminologist, was that Hamilton could have committed suicide by loosely draping a piece of twine across the front of her neck and by tying the ends to the door handle of her room, a method commonly used by the elderly.

The experts reasoned that Marion, who apparently had a fascination with knot-tying, was sitting against the door when she killed herself. As she toppled over, the twine was released. The rope could have moved further when Wilson opened the door and ambulance attendants entered the room.

Gardner theorized that Marion's progressive senility had been hastened by her mother's death. He had even located letters in which she articulated her unhappiness and discussed suicide. In an attempt to prove this, he had requested, when preparing for Elouise Wilson's trial in 1976, that Eunice Coote be exhumed to determine if her death was a murder. His theory was that Marion Hamilton had killed her mother and later was so remorseful that she killed herself.

Gardner went on a radio talk show with the venerable Jack Webster on May 29, 1978 to champion his theories. Webster, the king of West Coast "talking heads," didn't realize the microphones were still on during a commercial break, and he and Gardner made an unflattering suggestion about Wilson's second defence lawyer, James Sutherland. Sutherland subsequently sued and the result was a slander settlement of several thousand dollars.

The recovery of Eunice Coote proved unrevealing. "We exhumed the body of her mother in order to tell me whether there was possibly foul-play between Hamilton and the mother Coote," Gardner said during the program. "Unfortunately, and this goes to our establishment, there was never a proper autopsy of the mother at the time of that original burial and so when we exhumed the body ... we were trying to find out whether it [the neck] had been broken or not by means of strangulation. [The body, however,] was already rotted, to put it bluntly; but the things which did come out of that exhumation was strange because the body had been buried with a piece of string which was about the size of a noose and a couple of scissors which was buried in the back of the body." Why scissors? It's one more mystery no one ever figured out.

Gardner asked federal Justice Minister Jacques Flynn to grant Wilson's request for a new trial based on his suicide theory. While the Wilson defence team managed to have preliminary interviews with justice officials, they did not result in a re-opening of the case.

There were those in the media who were convinced Gardner had a brilliant case and others in the legal profession, such as prosecutor John Hall, who labelled the theory "bunk." Whatever its merits, Gardner's theory was controversial and got spectacular play in the British Columbia media. He seemed to genuinely believe that there had been a miscarriage of justice. "The miscarriage is unfortunate to say the least because in our system you would expect the adversary system to bring out all the evidence in a conflict-type manner before a court so the jury can make a proper decision based on all the evidence. In this case ... the main defence in my view never saw the light of day and the main defence, of course, was suicide. It was not even breathed in the courtroom."

Although her petition for a new trial didn't make it, Elouise Wilson somehow avoided being sent across the country to Kingston's Prison for Women, where the majority of convicted female Canadian killers are imprisoned. Instead, she was sent to Twin Maples, the women's minimum security institution at the Alouette River Correctional Centre in B.C. Almost 10 years later,

on May 29, 1987, she was paroled. She is living somewhere in British Columbia.

In the first interview since she was released, Elouise
said she is still hoping her case gets re-opened because of
"the gross miscarriage of justice." She has retained two
female lawyers and "they want to have the whole thing
cleared, they think it's all dreadful," she said, refusing to
name her counsel. "The whole trouble [with having it
re-opened] was the bad publicity." Elouise also wouldn't
say where in the province she was living, whether she was
using her real name or what type of life she had built for
herself because "when people meet me, myself, it's fine.
When they know my name, they get iced right off."

Reflecting on her prison experience, Elouise
described it as "dreadful. I could write the most horrible
book. The women who take drugs and that, they're the
most violent and horrible people. My faith saved me."

EIGHT

Anything for Erica

DETECTIVES Wayne Oldham and Neale Tweedy got the call from the duty inspector just before midnight. A man had been ambushed in Scarborough, just east of Toronto, Ont. while getting out of his car in an underground garage. Uniformed officers were at the scene, an apartment at 121 Trudelle St. and had already taken statements from the couple who first spotted the body. While two shots apparently had been fired, only one shell, a shotgun type, had been found on the floor of the man's black GMC Jimmy truck. No weapon was nearby, meaning it wasn't a suicide.

September 22, 1986 was a hell of a night to get called out. It was pouring rain and miserably cold, a night best reserved for comfortably snuggling in bed. Oldham and Tweedy quickly put on their suits, ties and trenchcoats at their respective homes and set out, looking more like two Bay Street lawyers than murder investigators. As detectives from Metro's homicide squad, Oldham and Tweedy knew two jobs had to be done immediately. The coroner had to be notified to pronounce the body dead and forensic experts brought in to collect evidence. When the pair arrived at the dusty underground garage in Scarborough, they observed the horror first-hand. The deceased, who looked in his mid-30s, had been shot at close range, once in the left cheek and a second time in the chest. Either one of the shots could have been fatal, Oldham surmised. "It was point blank and deliberately placed," he jotted down in his notes.

Apparently, the man had just pulled the keys out of the ignition and was leaving his truck when he was gunned down. The driver's door was still partly open. The interior light highlighted the dried brain tissue that splattered throughout the cab of the truck. The bullet blasts had pushed the man's body onto a plastic baby seat in the passenger's side of the front seat. "His head was in the baby seat," Tweedy said. "The first thing I wondered was if it was over the child."

Later, a post-mortem would reveal the killing in a more clinical fashion. The entrance wound on the left lateral chest was level with the nipple. The blast to the face entered to the front of the left ear, fracturing the skull and disengaging the upper jaw. An X-ray would show nine pellets in the right chest, five pellets in the head and three more medium-sized fragments in the head. The cause of death was shotgun wounds to the chest and head.

As messy as this murder was, Oldham and Tweedy

looked at the body with a feeling akin to detachment. Having already covered more than 90 murders between them, Oldham, 41, and Tweedy, 35, had developed that thick skin common to cops, crime reporters, and ambulance drivers. It's an important trait that allows police to make decisions in a methodical way, rather than emotionally.

The pair divided the chores. Tweedy would look after the immediate scene. He was in charge of the car, the garage, the body. He would ensure that the forensic evidence was collected properly and that nothing would be tampered with or overlooked. Oldham was in charge of information gathering. He wanted to "blitz" the murder. While the murder was still "fresh," saturation coverage would help him get the job done quickly and correctly.

Twelve uniformed officers began a door-to-door canvass of the complex of apartments, looking for anyone who may have heard or seen anything. Marine unit officers dived into nearby swimming pools to see if the murder weapon or weapons were there. All police forces in Ontario were alerted that a shotgun death had occurred and that extreme caution should be used when stopping vehicles with suspicious occupants in them.

In the meantime, Oldham had to find out what lifestyle and behaviour the murder victim had. "One question I kept asking myself is: 'What was this person doing that was so provocative that someone would want to kill him?'" Oldham said later in an interview. Looking inside the victim's wallet, the detectives discovered his name was Randall Carl Giesecke, 35. He was an insurance underwriter with Sunlife of Canada, a job that required him to work odd hours. He had greying brown hair and a bushy moustache. Flipping through the cellophane portion of Giesecke's wallet, Oldham and Tweedy noticed a picture of a smiling baby girl who, they eventually found out, was being babysat a few floors above. The detectives gazed at the picture for a moment. It must be his daughter, they thought. A kid without a father means that somewhere out there is a wife without a husband. Inside Giesecke's jacket pocket, the officers found rough notes scribbled on a piece of paper. It spelled out the details of a new life insurance policy for a Mike and Susan Simmons, two non-smokers who supposedly lived at 164 Hollyberry Trail in North York. Police would later discover there was no such address.

In canvassing 121 Trudelle, officers interviewed a couple whose apartment was directly above the shooting. They said they heard what sounded like a shot at about 7:15 p.m. Then they turned down the television and heard another shot. Police were now able to pin a time down to the murder.

Through checks, Oldham found out from Children's Aid that Randall Giesecke had been involved in a custody battle over his 17-month-old daughter, Erica. In fact, the custody hearing was scheduled to go to court on September 30, just eight days away. The mother's name was Harriet Renae Giesecke, born on May 15, 1946 in Detroit. According to Children's Aid, Mrs. Giesecke's chances of winning custody seemed slim. She was a parolee, had a record of writing bad cheques, and often signed herself into Toronto's Clarke Institute to receive psychiatric care. Custody then could be a motive but there was one thing that didn't fit. "Women really don't ambush an individual in a garage," Oldham said. Still, Harriet Giesecke seemed the strongest lead, and as it turned out, she was just five minutes away, living with her estranged husband's aunt, Yvonne Shannon.

Shortly after 6 a.m., Oldham and Tweedy called on the Shannon residence. The rain had stopped and the sun was rising. "We were in a very difficult position. Here we wanted to talk to a person who just lost her husband in a marriage that was full of hosility. If she's a suspect, she knows damn well what happened. We have to go in there treating her as a grieving widow. At the same time, we have to monitor her."

Mrs. Shannon answered a knock at the door. The detectives flashed their badges and told her they wished to speak to Harriet Giesecke. As they walked toward the kitchen, Harriet came up from the basement. She was an "earthy" woman with long, thick, ginger-coloured hair, fair skin, and eyes so dark they were almost black. "In the most compassionate way we know how, we gave her the message that her husband had been fatally shot," Oldham said.

Harriet screamed, thrashed about the house, and made a mournful noise that sounded like an animal in pain. Yet when Oldham met her eyes, there were no tears. Was it all an act? "I don't know how to explain it except to say they were very sinister looking eyes." Oldham had an unsettling feeling that something was very,

very wrong here. Despite the histrionics, Harriet's grief seemed more orchestrated than real. Certainly she didn't seem as devastated as Mrs. Shannon was.

Oldham knew a weak or inexperienced person who fires a shotgun usually ends up with a knuckle scrape from the gun's kick-back action. However, Harriet's fingers were as tender and pink as they come. If she hadn't pulled the trigger, who had? Was there an accomplice?

As Harriet sat down, he memorized the tread of her shoe. This would be important, he thought. Forensic experts from the Ontario Provincial Police were "electrostating" the garage to collect footprints. "We get a sheet of plastic substance and run an electric charge and it makes an imprint adhere to the sheet," Oldham explained. "It will bring up footwear impressions invisible to the human eye." Unfortunately, the uniformed officers who had responded to the first call didn't know of this technique and had trampled all over the scene. While the electrostating worked properly, all it picked up were the bootprints of police officers.

In the meantime, Harriet explained how she had spent her night. She had gone out in the early evening, then returned to the Shannon residence where, at 10 p.m., she took a call from her family lawyer, Marvin Shiffman. She went to sleep shortly thereafter. The detectives jotted all this down but they had a creepy feeling they couldn't shake. "There's something wrong. She's in there, she's dirty," Oldham later told Tweedy, who nodded in agreement. They left the Shannon house with the gnawing feeling that Harriet Giesecke knew exactly what had happened in the underground garage on Trudelle St.

Oldham and Tweedy went back to the murder scene and told the uniformed cops to call the victim's mother and stepfather to have them come to the victim's apartment. Although they were certain the dead man was Randall Giesecke, they needed the body identified by next-of-kin. The detectives then took the elevator to Randall Giesecke's ninth-floor apartment. Inside, there was a colourful nursery, filled with pictures of Erica, toys, clothes, books, and a mobile. "There was a sensitivity in that place you normally expect from a woman," Tweedy would remark later.

When Giesecke's mother and stepfather arrived at the apartment, they were eager to talk. They spoke of their son's tortured, volatile relationship with the former Harriet Pollack. A homemaker from Southfield, Michigan, near Detroit, Pollack had met Randall, a coach of Toronto's Young Nationals hockey team, in 1982 in Chicago where her two sons, aged 10 and 13, were playing hockey for a team from Detroit. Randall was married at the time to "a classy, lovely, intelligent woman" named Wendy, according to Tweedy, but the insurance underwriter was unhappy with the relationship. Soon Harriet and Giesecke began an affair, carrying on their clandestine liaisons in London, Ont. motels. It was a relationship founded on lies, according to friends. Randall was a high-liver who, at the start of their involvement, apparently told Harriet he had a lot of money and was separated. Neither was true: he regularly spent beyond his means and was still very much married to Wendy Giesecke. At the same time, Harriet told Randall that her mother was rich. In fact, Harriet was a parolee who had done time for fraud, theft and possession. Any money she got was from writing phoney cheques. She was, however, divorced and her ex-husband, Ernest, had custody of their two boys.

After almost a year of clandestine motel rendezvous, Harriet and Randall married at the Scarborough Civic Centre wedding chapel on November 20, 1983, just five days after he had divorced his wife. Randall wanted a child and seventeen months after the marriage, Harriet gave birth in April 1985 to Erica Ashley. But their happiness together was shortlived. There were loud arguments over money, and Harriet claimed Randall was beating her. Three months after the birth of Erica, the parents were estranged. Giesecke's mother and stepfather "portrayed to us a very scurrilous, sinister individual," Oldham said. "Instead of diminishing our suspicion, they start enhancing it and we're starting to get pretty high on her."

Harriet Giesecke at first didn't realize she was under suspicion for her husband's murder. In fact, the chatty suspect telephoned the detectives to tell them to keep her informed of the latest developments. She seemed to fancy herself as being one step ahead of the cops. It was an attitude Oldham and Tweedy wanted her to have.

Giesecke's ignorance didn't last long, however. One day "I'm on the phone to her parole officer," Tweedy recalled, "and she puts Harriet on the phone to me. She [Harriet] talks about how upset she is and how she's fearing for her child's life." Tweedy wanted to keep his suspect on the line long enough to permit surveillance officers to get to where she was and follow her. As the widow and the detective kept chatting, it gradually dawned on Harriet Giesecke that *she* was a suspect. With this realization, she hung up the phone, then curled into a fetal position on the office floor. "She said something to the parole officer to the effect that 'that bastard or that fucker will never put this one on me.'"

On the day of Randall Giesecke's funeral, six intelligence officers tracked his widow to Edwards Gardens on Lawrence Avenue and Leslie Street in North York, where they saw her strolling hand in hand with a Bruce Bernard Lynch. The couple sat on a park bench and he placed his head on her lap. Like a scene out of a romance novel, she would lean down and passionately kiss him and run her fingers through his hair. Clearly, she was devastated by her estranged husband's death.

Lynch's background was a checkered one. Now 25, he'd been in and out of prison since age 14 for robbery offences. He was currently out on parole after being sentenced to six years' imprisonment for a 1982 trust company hold-up in North Bay. He had recently pleaded guilty to holding up The Bay in Oshawa. Prior to being sentenced, Lynch was at the Clarke Institute of Psychiatry in Toronto undergoing a psychiatric assessment.

The detectives also visited the Clarke, where they encountered a few people who knew Harriet, who frequently checked herself into the hospital. She was called "Ma Barker" and her "boys" were Lynch and Ron Nicoll, a seasoned criminal and alcoholic, who had spent much of his life in psychiatric hospitals. At the end of August, a nurse found Harriet and Bruce in a "compromising position." The nurse, Leonard Rose, was doing his regular checks through the forensic unit of the hospital at 7:00 that August morning when he discovered Bruce Lynch was not in his bed. Rose looked in the men's washroom and the women's washroom but couldn't locate him. He made his way to room 401 and Harriet Giesecke wasn't in bed either. Peering between the beds, Rose saw a pair of white, quivering knees, spread apart. A closer inspection revealed a man locked between the knees, thrusting his pelvis.

"Stop it now!" Rose shouted. The man turned to look at Rose. It was Bruce Lynch. Hesitantly, he withdrew from the embrace. Harriet stayed on the floor, not fazed by the surprise visit, but apparently satisfied. Two days later, Giesecke signed herself out of the hospital.

The only other person in the Clarke Institute who seemed to know Harriet as intimately as Lynch was Nicoll. He would later testify that he had sex with Harriet Giesecke twice in the backseat of a car. Harriet, he said, wanted to "shack up" with him and had offered to pay him $5,000 to murder her husband. Nicoll wasn't a bad choice for a killer: included in his criminal resume was a total of 17 years spent behind bars for crimes including assault causing bodily harm and robbery with violence. He said he was sitting in the Clarke with Harriet and Lynch one afternoon, each talking about their respective prison histories when she said: "I've got two guys here from prison. How would you guys like to kill my husband?" Nicoll thought she was kidding and began to laugh. Lynch made no expression. She explained that her mother sent her blank cheques in the mail so she could afford it. Nicoll said he would need the money to move if he did it and she said: "Ronny, I'll give you $5,000 to shoot Randy." Harriet explained that while she knew she would never get custody of Erica, she was determined that her ex-husband wouldn't either.

For the next week Harriet and Nicoll talked about the murder and how it would be set up. He suggested that she take off with the baby but she explained that the authorities would come after her. It was around this time, in mid-August of 1986, that Nicoll noticed Harriet and Lynch were becoming much, well…closer. Nicoll decided to back away. Later, he read newspaper accounts of the murder of Randall Giesecke. After talking about it with his ex-common-law wife and a Salvation Army major, he realized he should go to police. He admitted that he had thought seriously about killing the insurance underwriter. Harriet had told him some maundering story about how she had been battered by her estranged husband. Nicoll figured it was no loss to the world to kill the clod. Then he realized it was wrong. His confession was a godsend to police.

In the meantime, other evidence was building to implicate Harriet Giesecke. A cashier supervisor from Le Baron Outdoor Products at Newtonbrook Plaza in Metro Toronto said a woman, later identified as Harriet, had come in looking for a high-powered magnum gun and ammunition to hunt big game the day before the Giesecke killing. A real estate agent in the same mall said

she, too, had seen Harriet that day, accompanied by a
man. Catherine McLean, a kindergarten teacher who
lived in the same apartment as Randall Giesecke, identified Harriet out of a photograph lineup as the woman she
saw driving a car into the apartment's underground
garage. She placed her there at 6:15 that night – about
one hour before Randall was shot.

A search of a basement apartment that Harriet and
Bruce had rented on Hollyberry Trail in North York had
uncovered a saw. Police suspected the saw may have been
used to "cut down" the shotgun used to kill Giesecke. An
officer was sent to the apartment with a giant magnet to
pick up any metal filings.

Matters seemed well in hand when the unexpected
happened: Bruce decided to make a move out of town.
After being caught having sex at the Clarke, Bruce faced
the prospect of getting a bad pre-sentence report relating
to his previous robbery charges. On September 3, he fled
the Clarke. Eight days later, he and Harriet moved into
the basement apartment on Hollyberry Trail. The day of
the funeral, September 25, Lynch split town. Police followed the robber west, down Highway 401. When Lynch
got to a Petro Canada gas station at Cambridge, Sergeant
Paul Byer walked up to Lynch's car, aimed a shotgun at
him, and yelled "police." Without saying a word, Lynch
got out, put his hands on the car and stayed silent. He was
charged with escaping custody and unlawful possession
of an automobile. Byer searched Lynch and the car. He
found two telephone numbers – one was that of Harriet's
mother – scribbled on a piece of paper.

During the drive back to Toronto, Lynch told Byer that he had been renting a basement apartment and had been working as a pizza deliveryman. Yes, he had been to the Clarke and to his father's Huntsville farm where he had stolen some tools. And yes, he knew Harriet Giesecke. He had met her at the Clarke and yes, he knew her husband had been murdered. He said he had been at his basement apartment at the time of the killing. The day after, Harriet would tell him her husband had been shot in an underground garage. Later, Lynch would tell Oldham and Tweedy in an interview that he felt like he was "going down for 25 years" and he didn't even know the man.

"Well, why would you go down for 25 years when you didn't do it?"

"She's smarter than me," Lynch replied.

"What's that got to do with it?" asked Oldham.

"She'll walk and I'll get 25 years."

"You didn't answer the question," Oldham pressed. "Why would you get 25 years and she'll walk if you didn't do it?"

"Cause I'm the bait."

Lynch also said Giesecke was such a clever manipulator that she had managed to get something "going on" between her and her psychiatrist at the Clarke Institute. "She's [his] pet. She does whatever she wants." (While Giesecke desperately tried to create the impression she was having a relationship with her psychiatrist that went beyond the doctor-patient norm, this innuendo was later found out to be unwarranted).

On Monday, November 24, 1986 – slightly more than two months after her estranged husband's death – Harriet was charged with first-degree murder in Scarborough. At the time of her arrest, she wanted to know three things: Was she was the only one being charged? Had police found the gun? What evidence did the police have?

"Well," said Tweedy, "you have the motive to kill Randy and it's just before the custody hearing."

"Go on."

"We know you were living with Bruce Lynch up until the time of the murder at 155 Hollyberry Trail . We think it's more than coincidence that Randy received fictitious information to go to 164 Hollyberry Trail that evening, right across the street."

"Anything else?"

"We know you lied about the movements on the day of the murder."

"Sergeant Tweedy, am I sick? Could I have been involved in this and not know? Could I have blanked it from my mind? [My doctor] said I was withdrawing. So there really is evidence that I did it?"

"That's why we charged you and that evidence will be fairly put before the court."

The next day Lynch was charged with first-degree murder at Millhaven Institution, where he had been serving time for two hold-ups.

Lynch was very reluctant to talk about Harriet and said he couldn't discuss the murder because a woman and child were involved. In a moment of self-realization, he said there was something "wrong" with him and the 12

Bible classes he had taken had only helped a bit. He said he was doing life imprisonment on the installment plan.

Here is the murder scenario as the police conceived it: Harriet, knowing she would never get custody of her child, wanted her estranged husband killed. At first, she and Lynch planned to kill Giesecke across the street from Lynch's basement apartment. To lure him there, they set up a phoney insurance policy appointment at a fictitious address. Then, realizing they would never get away with the murder in the open, they called and cancelled the phoney appointment. Since they knew Randall would likely return home that evening, Harriet drove a silver Honda Civic that Lynch had stolen from an ex-girlfriend in Kingston in early September. With Lynch lying in the backseat, she parked it next to Randall's spot and awaited his arrival.

When Giesecke did arrive, Lynch grabbed the loaded shotgun and swung into action. "The keys were still in his [Giesecke's] hand, he put one foot on the ground and was about to step out," Tweedy theorized. "Bruce Lynch pointed a shotgun at him and shot him in the chest and shredded his heart like spaghetti. Then he got closer and put a hole in his head. It was the size of a golfball."

This scenario was put to the test when the trial opened in May 1988 in Ontario Supreme Court with Mr. Justice Archie Campbell presiding. John Rosen represented Lynch, Ed Schofield acted for Giesecke, and John McMahon for the Crown attorney's office.

Outlining the case, McMahon noted that Randall

Giesecke's life was insured for $200,000 and that Erica was named as beneficiary. Married in 1983, Harriet and Randall had had financial problems within months of their nuptials. Prior to the birth of daughter Erica in 1985, Harriet was charged with several fraud-related charges stemming, in part, from the issuance of bad cheques. Randall Giesecke had signed as a guarantor to ensure his wife would not have to stay in police custody.

Three months after Erica's birth, Randall Giesecke left his wife, taking the baby with him. What followed was a bitter custody battle. In August, he was granted interim custody and obtained a [restraining] court order forbidding Harriet from taking the baby out of Ontario. Harriet subsequently applied to the Supreme Court and was given access to Erica on Tuesdays and Fridays. Harriet had visits with her baby at the Shannon home where the father would drop off the baby. Harriet subsequently got an acquaintance to follow Randall home. He told Harriet her estranged husband lived at 121 Trudelle St. Did the apartment, by chance, have an underground parking lot? she enquired.

While this custody battle raged, Immigration Canada ordered Giesecke to be deported back to the United States because she had worked illegally at two Toronto law firms. Also, in February 1986, she had been given a nine-month jail sentence on the fraud-related charges. She served three months in the Toronto West Detention Centre before being paroled.

One of the more bizarre moments in the seven-week murder trial occurred when it seemed Giesecke's counsel might be called as a witness. During a *voir dire,* Crown attorney John McMahon said he had learned from homicide detectives that a letter existed which supposedly implicated Bruce Lynch in the killing. (Harriet's psychiatrist at the Clarke Institute learned of the mystery letter and mentioned it to detectives during an interview. The police, in turn, queried McMahon).

Ed Schofield, Giesecke's lawyer, now had the original letter which, he believed, was written in a code he hoped he and the psychiatrist might be able to decipher. The letter, reportedly penned by Lynch, was apparently confessional in nature, and not addressed.

When the trial got underway, McMahon said that if Schofield did not voluntarily present the letter in court, the Crown would ask that it be seized, or failing that, that Ed Schofield be subpoenaed to testify at the trial.

Both options irked Schofield. He had shown the letter to the psychiatrist in confidence but unfortunately the psychiatrist didn't understand it that way. Moreover, it had not been signed, nor was it addressed to anyone. Eventually, Judge Campbell ruled that "the document in question be placed in a sealed envelope in the custody of the court, bearing the order of the court in the form of an endorsement that the envelope is not to be opened without an order of a judge of this court or the Court of Appeal on notice to both accused and Mr. Schofield and the Crown."

Finally, the woman everyone had been waiting for

took the stand. Harriet Giesecke's testimony revealed a woman of exceptional intelligence, well-prepared for the rigorous cross-examination. The accused murderer told her lawyer she wanted to tell her side of the story. "She had an amazing memory," said McMahon. "She'd know each and every page of the court brief."

Giesecke stuck to her alibi for the night of her estranged husband's death. She had been nowhere near the Trudelle Street apartment. And Bruce Lynch? Well, she testified, a few weeks before the trial he confessed to killing Randall, albeit accidentally.

Her eyes watering, Giesecke said she would never have wanted her estranged husband dead. "I never, ever would have taken her [Erica's] father away from her."

Lynch, she said, acted on his own but out of love for her. "He felt he could talk to Randall, threaten him, scare him, tell him to back off" the custody battle. However, the insurance underwriter only "laughed at him, told him to go fly a kite." When he grabbed at the shotgun Lynch was carrying, it went off in a "reflex action," she said Lynch had told her. Worried that Giesecke might be able to identify him, "he had to make sure he was dead so he shot him a second time."

According to Harriet, Lynch said he "panicked over what he had done" and fled the underground garage. Later, he placed the shotgun and the clothes he'd been wearing into a shopping bag and pitched it into Lake Ontario. After he confessed to her, Harriet said he "wanted me to forgive him." But she was steely in her response. "You took her father."

The accused went on to deny Ron Nicoll's testimony that she had offered him $5,000 to eliminate her husband. "I did not have $5,000 to offer."

McMahon retorted there was no other motive Nicoll would have for such a story other than the truth. Harriet gave him one: "I believe I brushed him off and he didn't like it." She denied Nicoll's claim of sexual involvement with her, saying it happened "only in his mind." She did agree that she had occasionally jokingly referred to herself and Lynch as "Bonnie and Clyde" because her lover had been involved in a bank robbery. But she denied Nicoll's testimony she was known as "Ma Barker" in the psychiatric hospital. Harriet also denied having sexual relations with another man at the Clarke, even though she wrote him a letter that asked, "Can we only hug or kiss, or are we allowed to do more?"

In his cross-examination, Lynch's lawyer, John Rosen, accused Harriet of fabricating her story. What she had given the court wasn't the truth but "the performance of a lifetime."

"It wasn't a performance; it was the truth," she snapped. "You just don't want to hear it." She repeatedly denied Rosen's suggestions that she had made up the story to "extricate" herself from a murder charge. "I don't need to be extricated, Mr. Rosen. I had nothing to do with it." At the same time, she acknowledged, "I bear a great guilt myself. No matter how it happened, my daughter will grow up without a father because of someone I lived with."

Rosen told Giesecke that her story made no sense and

"this was nothing but a cold-blooded ambush of your husband. He was taken by surprise and didn't have a chance."

Replied Harriet, "I'm only repeating a story that your client told me. I want the truth to be known."

Rosen did not call Lynch to testify. "I had planned all along not to call evidence," Rosen said later in an interview. "It was bad enough the jury had to hear his background. To put him on the stand would to be reinforce that bad aspect." Instead, the defence of his client extended to pointing the finger at Lynch's co-accused.

During closing addresses, McMahon told the jurors that if they used their common sense, they could come to only one conclusion – that Lynch and Giesecke were responsible for the killing. He labelled Giesecke's finger-pointing as the "defence of desperation." He described Harriet as "the one with the brains and the motive" while Lynch was "the triggerman. The two accused go together like fingers in a glove," he said, adding that Lynch was in love with her and was prepared to do anything for her, including kill her husband.

Harriet's lawyer told the jurors that Nicoll's evidence was "totally useless garbage" that should not be believed. He conceded that although some of the evidence in the case may raise suspicions against Harriet, it "does not go over the threshold" of proof beyond a reasonable doubt that she is guilty.

Rosen argued that while his client, Bruce Lynch, may have learned what happened to Randall Giesecke, " he wasn't a party to it because he wasn't there" and as a result is not guilty of murder. He reminded the jurors that

Lynch had told police "I was at home when her husband was killed [and] I didn't know [about it] until the next day...." He quoted Kipling to the jurors: "The female of the species is more deadly than the male."

Rosen's arguments didn't appear to bother Harriet. Indeed, she seemed to think an acquittal was on the horizon. This amazing self-assurance was revealed when she told an officer who was unlocking her handcuffs on the way into court: "This is the last time you'll be putting these cuffs on me."

But after the jury deliberated for over four days, Harriet Giesecke was astonished when, on June 18, 1988, she was found guilty of first-degree murder. Lynch was acquitted. Obviously, the jury did not believe the police theory that Lynch was the triggerman.

Harriet Giesecke is currently serving a life sentence in Kingston's Penitentiary for Women (P4W), with no eligibility for parole for 25 years. She is appealing her case but it has not been heard in court yet. Bruce Lynch is serving a 10-year sentence for robbery and theft at Joyceville Penitentiary, also in Kingston. The pair wed in June 1989 in P4W's chapel. Every six weeks, corrections guards bring Bruce to a trailer on the P4W grounds where they have a "normal life." Erica, a pretty happy girl, is seven years old and living with Randall's parents in Toronto. They applied for and received custody of the girl.

If the saying that truth is stranger than fiction is true, then Harriet's and Bruce's marriage is a shining example.

Although she had accused Bruce of murdering her husband at the trial, they have what she calls a "wonderful relationship." Bruce seems to bear no ill against her. The couple are in love; they give each other sex and moral support, and Bruce will be out of prison much sooner than Harriet. Knowing she will have a supportive husband on the outside must be a comforting thought for a woman who will be trapped behind bars for another two decades.

In October 1990 Harriet met with this author in P4W. Wearing a Mickey Mouse T-shirt and blue sweatpants and looking years younger than her 40-plus age, she talked of her life in prison since her arrest in 1986. For the suburban homemaker with an education from Eastern Michigan and Wayne State universities, Kingston has been tough. But then again, Harriet is a survivor. She spoke of her close alliances with many of the women doing time for murder and manslaughter in P4W.

Harriet hasn't been a model prisoner during her stay. Like most, she has her good days and bad ones. On occasion she has been segregated for causing trouble. She takes sewing classes and hopes she can get a new trial. To this day, she fancies herself a clever manipulator and something of a vixen.

"It was stupid for him [Randall] to die, there was no reason for him to die," she says tearfully. Harriet doesn't come right out and deny she killed Giesecke; she just says she has never admitted to it.

If she were to have killed her estranged husband, she says, she would have packed up his apartment and made it look like he left town. After she killed him, she would have dumped his body in a place they would never find it. "If they don't have a body, they can't get you."

What she genuinely does feel, however, is sad regret that she hasn't had contact with her daughter in four years. Not a picture, not a phone call. But who can blame Giesecke's parents for that?

NINE

Love and Death

PHILLIP Francis Power was an authoritative, all-consuming man. He looked as much like a heavyweight champ as a union president. His burly physique served as an intimidating tool when negotiating with management for the Canadian Union of Postal Workers in Halifax. Yet, for all his seeming strength, by the spring of 1985, Power had made a colossal mess of his life. His marriage was over, he had resigned from his job as union president and he had become deeply involved with his estranged wife's younger sister, a woman 13 years his junior. It was a relationship that would eventually cost him his life.

Lisa Melva MacDonald, a petite brunette, first met Power when she was only nine. He was 22 and going out with one of Lisa's older sisters, Betty. In 1978 Power and Betty wed. The Lisa-Phil relationship at first had the cast of baby sister/older brother and he often took her along with Betty on outings to the movies, picnics and festivals.

Their relationship became more serious – and sexual – in 1984 while Power was still married to Betty MacDonald. This involvement, however, broke off soon after it started, when Lisa fell in love with another man. Whatever chance at happiness that brief relationship may have had was snuffed out when the man was killed in an automobile accident. The sadness and depression threw Lisa into Power's arms once again.

Lisa Macdonald was born June 27, 1965 in Halifax to a Catholic family consisting of eight brothers and seven sisters, ranging in age from 18 to 42. She was the thirteenth child. MacDonald's father, Lewis, was described as "an alcoholic who sexually abused her older sisters and physically abused her brothers," according to a court report. From the age of seven to 11, MacDonald was treated better because her father wasn't drinking as heavily. He died in a car accident in 1976.

It was, as a psychiatrist would later say, "a chaotic home situation." In having to negotiate a world of abuse, both sexual and physical, alcoholism and "a strong history of psychiatric illness on the paternal side of her family," it was hardly any wonder that Lisa MacDonald developed "a pattern of emotional instability" as she grew up.

It was no coincidence that Lisa, who says she also was sexually abused as a youngster, had sought out Power. She attributed losing her fear of sex to Power's loving touch but, unwittingly, Lisa fell into the same cycle of abuse she detested as a child.

A man with aqua blue eyes and salt and pepper hair,

Power knew how to charm MacDonald and make her feel safe. President of CUPW since 1980, he was known for his aggressive style when negotating on behalf of the 22,000 members of the region, which included Halifax, Dartmouth, Bedford and Sackville, Nova Scotia. Power hated the bureaucracy and mundane paperwork and the hearings that went with being a union boss but grudgingly motored through them. "He was very worker-oriented," said one woman on the executive. "He was always ready to defend the workers, day or night. He was not into the officialdom of the union, he was more of a worker's worker."

He held the presidency for four years. Then suddenly, in 1984, he announced that he would not be seeking re-election – something that threw a wrench into the plans of the executive. Apparently, he was a shoo-in for another four-year term. The local tried to persuade him to stay but Power would have none of it. He meekly accepted the job of a wicket clerk at a local Canada Post office.

By the spring of 1985 Power's six-year marriage to Betty MacDonald was foundering and the couple separated. Lisa MacDonald and Power soon set up home together in the modest surroundings of the Sackville Manor Trailer Park. At first, the relationship seemed warm and they got along well. She was completing Grade 12 at Sackville High School and taking a bartender's course in Dartmouth. But, within months, Lisa's relationship with Power became "chaotic, unsettled, and disturbing."

One time he grabbed her by her throat, rammed her

head into a closet door, and punched her in the chest. The force of his blows tore her neck muscles and she had to go to a doctor in Bedford, a bedroom community of 10,000 located 15 km outside Halifax.

Lisa, however, didn't consider laying charges against her lover or of leaving him. "I stayed with him because I loved him. He apologized and said it wouldn't happen again." However, it happened at least five more times. One of those times, after Lisa had accidentally tripped over a television cord, he threw MacDonald against a door and held her up by her face.

Still, Lisa hung on. "He kept saying it was his nerves. I was trying to be a good wife and stick by him."

Alongside the violence came propositions of "strange" sex. "He wanted me to sleep with other people," she would say later. "He liked kinky sex," liked the idea of watching his woman in the company of others. Repulsed, Lisa refused. By the summer of 1985, she was heading toward a nervous breakdown and checked herself into the Nova Scotia Hospital in Dartmouth, a bridge away from Halifax. MacDonald spent a month there, trying to get herself together. Upon her release she moved in with another older sister, Theresa, and vowed never to see Power again. Her resolve lasted close to six months, as she resisted the constant barrage of blandishments and love letters from the burly ex-union leader. Finally, in December, she broke down. "I was still in love with him and he made a lot of promises. He asked me to marry him." As well, Power promised to have no contact with his estranged wife.

Alas, life with Power was no better the second time

around. For reasons unknown, Power quit his job as a wicket clerk and he picked up jobs as they came. Lisa took a seven-month training course as a nurse's aide. But she didn't like nursing-home work and was eventually hired at a Burger King. After that she held a raft of jobs, each one seemingly more low paying and dead-end than its predecessor. The couple moved from one Sackville-area apartment to another, rarely putting their things in order before having to leave again. They finally moved into a rooming house on Barrington Street, a derelict area undergoing major renovations, and stayed there for seven months. Eventually they were forced to go on social assistance to make ends meet. MacDonald became upset that they were unable to find a stable, quiet environment in which to live while Power became increasingly depressed and despondent. He gambled obsessively and failed to scrape enough money together for clothes or even food. As their financial problems grew so did Power's temper and possessiveness.

He wanted MacDonald to stay home most of the time and forbade her from seeing her friends and family. He wanted complete control over her life. MacDonald felt torn between wanting to be accepted by her family and her longing for Power's love. "There was no life with him and there was no life with my family."

Sadly, Lisa MacDonald had been disowned by most of her family when they discovered she had been dating Power on the sly since 1984. Power's wife, Betty, had at first been unaware of this involvement but she sensed that something was wrong. Is there someone else? she asked. No, said her husband. There's only you. We're just having a rough spell right now. When Betty found out the truth from the gossip mill, she was devastated.

Power's involvement with Lisa had been the talk of the town for some time but no one had had the heart to tell Betty at first. Maybe it wasn't true, some thought. Perhaps Power and the younger MacDonald were just friends. Eventually, those knowing glances between Power and MacDonald, the cheshire cat smiles, the giddy conversations, the sparks that flew when they talked made their relationship one of the worst-kept secrets in Halifax.

Some of the more judgmental folk scolded the petite MacDonald for stealing the man away. But those with a more objective eye saw the situation for what it was: Power was a predatory man who had seduced a naive, vulnerable, troubled girl 13 years his junior and filled her head with false promises. Building on the trusting relationship he had made with her as a child, he leapt to the unforgivable step of seduction.

Interestingly, Power was not altogether comfortable in this role. Two months after he and Betty split up, he apparently suffered an attack of separation anxiety and suddenly decided he wanted his wife back. They tried to make it work for several weeks but she couldn't forget what had happened. "I thought I could but I couldn't … I was getting bitter and I didn't think it would work out. I couldn't forget what had happened." Every time Betty MacDonald tried to make a step towards fixing their broken marriage, she was overwhelmed by images of Lisa with her husband. Soon, that was all she could think about. Hurt, resentful, she saw her life coming down to one of two choices: live with the "background noise" of a past relationship that tortured her, or get rid of Power. The decision, while gutwrenching, was obvious: Betty told Phil Power to leave. Power was not happy: "He wanted to try, he didn't want us to split up at that point." Yet for all his resistance to Betty's wishes, Power, unlike with the younger sister, never laid a hand on Betty.

Was it possible that Phil Power was in love with both women? Or was he merely out to meet his own needs and failing to ponder the damage he was doing to them?

Clearly there was no grand scheme to make these two sisters miserable. Power was acting completely on emotion, hormones, and a lust for power. The glue that had kept his life successful and "normal" for years – a steady job, a wife, respect from his colleagues – now seemed to bore him. His path to self-destruction began with his self-centeredness. Wanting to indulge his "badness," he came to wallow, then drown in it. By the late eighties he was incapable of loving anyone, including himself.

Amazingly, through all this, Lisa MacDonald continued to hold onto her fragile faith. But by the fall of 1987 she was severely depressed and penning suicide notes. One was addressed to "Anyone Who Still Cares." In it she said, "How could he make things so miserable when he said he's made them so beautiful and happy?" she wrote. "Please come to my funeral, Phil. Goodbye." Power quickly responded with a loving note that convinced MacDonald to change her mind. "May your life be blessed with the same happiness you brought me," he said.

Still, there was no respite from bad news. Doctors,

concerned about an irregularity in MacDonald's pap smear, discovered a large cyst, later determined to be cancerous. "I had blood clots and I couldn't get medication because Phillip took the welfare cheque and went to Sydney," where his mother lived.

A desperate Lisa went looking for him there, irrationally concerned he might not have a place to stay. "I figured I wasn't worth anything and even if he was that bad to me, I couldn't be that bad to him. I didn't want him to be sleeping in the cold." The more she looked, the more depressed she became. She called up social services in an attempt to get money for medication, then she decided "to say goodbye and commit suicide," she said.

When she did connect with Power in Halifax he promised he would see a psychiatrist for his problems and asked MacDonald to stay with him. "I said it would be better if we split up. He could stay at his mother's [in Sydney] and [he] would be better off." Power told MacDonald he loved her and desperately wanted to be with her. He had plans to get a cabdriver's licence and start a new life in Sydney. Power asked her to be part of his new life. Lisa declined but nonetheless agreed to drive with him to Sydney. When they arrived, he wanted to make love but she didn't. "He cried and said he didn't want to fight anymore, that he loved me."

A distraught MacDonald hopped on a bus for Halifax. "Through the bus window I saw him running, saying, 'I love you, I love you.'" Getting into his car, Power drove alongside the bus until he could no longer keep up, all the while shouting three words that had been bandied about so often they were now meaningless.

Upon Lisa's return to her Halifax rooming-house, Power unleashed a stream of collect phone calls. "He wanted to come back with me. He was giving me instructions that 'you couldn't do anything without me.'" "Life," he said, "could, would be beautiful. The future will be brighter. Believe me. Believe in us."

Lisa listened patiently at first, then snapped. "I can't afford these calls, just say what you have to say," she screamed. "I've decided I'm going to kill myself. It's my choice. You don't have to feel guilty about anything. Good-bye."

MacDonald went to a tavern with the intention of "drinking herself to death" but all she did was get drunk on beer and sad at heart. Power called her, again, convinced she had tried to slit her wrists but "I told him I hadn't." Within days Power was back in Halifax and living with Lisa. MacDonald's mother gave her some good, harsh advice. "You're stupid, Lisa. You're letting him play you for a sucker. You've got to end it."

Power, of course, did not change. He spent much of his time trying to turn MacDonald against people in town, feeding her lies and paranoid theories in an attempt to control her every move. "He tried to turn me against my mother," MacDonald said.

On October 11, 1987, "he told me to make sure the housework was done but I was just totally exhausted." MacDonald took a nap. When she awoke she began to clean again. She picked up a file laying on a desk, and a letter fell out. On it, in Power's hand-writing, was a list of things to do, one of which was to write to Betty MacDonald. Lisa MacDonald was livid. After all his protestations to the contrary, Phil Power, it seemed, wanted to see his ex-wife.

Lisa felt she had to talk to Power, "but if I do that I might get in a fight and I'm afraid of what I'll do." Distraught, she decided to seek help at Nova Scotia Hospital, where she had spent time in 1985. She tried to put together a night bag but didn't have the concentration for it. She ran out onto the street. Realizing she had no money, she remembered she had an instant-teller card with her. She headed for Spring Garden Road in Halifax to an automatic banking machine but before she arrived, she spotted Power in his car. "I yelled at him [but] he kept driving by." Figuring he hadn't seen her, she had just started on her way again when "he came around the corner. I didn't know if I should talk to him or go to the hospital."

MacDonald decided not to talk. "I figured we'd get into a fight in the street. I said: 'I have to go to the hospital in Dartmouth.'"

"What's wrong, baby? What's wrong?" Power pleaded.

"I will show you what's wrong," MacDonald shot back. She pulled out the offending letter. "What's this? You're not supposed to know her number."

Power mumbled some feeble explanations but she knew she had him cold.

"Why are you lying to me? Why are you doing this to me again?"

Power tried to calm her down, and managed to get her to sit in the front passenger seat of his station wagon.

"I was shaking my head," MacDonald recalled. "I

said, 'I don't know what's going on.'" The next thing she remembered, Power was asking her what had happened.

"I didn't pay any attention to him," she said. "He opened up one side of his jacket and I saw blood. Then I turned around and there was a knife in my hand."

David Marriott was eating a Sunday Chinese dinner just after 5:30 p.m. on October 11 at the Garden View Restaurant when a frantic woman, her eyes wide with terror, burst into the room. There was blood on one of her hands. "He's dead, he's dead," the woman screamed. "He's dead, he's dead!" Then she ran off.

Marriott and his daughter's boyfriend followed her, thinking they might be able to help. They got to a station wagon where they saw the woman climb into the passenger side. At this point, "I saw the gentleman laying with his head back, in the driver's seat," Marriott would later testify. "I opened the [driver's side] door and I sort of put my head inside the car and I pulled it out quite quickly because there was a Doberman Pinscher dog in the station wagon."

The dog – Phil Power's pet – seemed friendly, however, so Marriott stuck his head back in the car and got a closer look at the victim. Power was still fastened in his seatbelt. "His eyes sort of rolled back in his head and when I reached down to unfasten the seatbelt, I noticed the blood on his shirt."

Marriott told his daughter's boyfriend to call an ambulance. Another bystander proceeded to calm Lisa

MacDonald, whose body was racked by sobs in the front seat. Suddenly, Power gained semi-consciousness. Raising his head he asked Marriott: "What's happening? I don't understand." Then he lost conciousness. That hazy statement would be Power's last earthly utterance.

Within five minutes, an ambulance pulled up. The attendant asked Marriott what happened and he replied that he really didn't know.

The ambulance attendant looked at the sobbing Lisa. "Lady," he hollered, "you've got to tell me what happened so I can try to help him."

Lisa replied: "We were arguing and I stabbed him." A bloodied steak knife was later found on the car floor.

They started to remove Power from the car as MacDonald continued to cry uncontrollably. "I did it," she sobbed. "How could I?" It would be a question she would ask herself every waking morning in her jail cell.

Power, his skin a blue pallor, was whisked to the trauma unit of Victoria General Hospital. He had been stabbed in the heart. Doctors decided an emergency thoracotonomy was in order to find out where the bleeding was. The doctors sliced through the chest wall and peeled back the skin and saw a massive blood clot. They removed it. They pulled Power's heart out of his chest and massaged it. Despite their exhaustive efforts, it wasn't enough, and Phillip Francis Power died at 6:28 that night.

Lisa MacDonald was on the scene and it fell to Corporal Kenny Bennett of the Halifax police to give her the bad – or good? – news. Although heavily medicated, she remained distraught and anxious, fearing the worst. She looked up at Bennett, his kind, sky-blue eyes surrounded by a weathered, ruddy complexion. His morose look told her enough. "I finally told her he passed away," Bennett said. "She wanted to see him but really she wasn't up to it."

Bennett then told her she would be charged with second-degree murder. This prompted another explosion of tears and she went on to explain how she suffered from premenstrual syndrome, which sometimes caused her to do crazy acts. The stabbing, she said, occurred one day before she was due to menstruate. "It seems like every time I go nuts, it's the day before my period," she said later. "People with PMS seem like they're crazy."

When she reached the interview room at the police station, she became hysterical again. "Please take me to the hospital, please I want to see him," she repeated again and again, wrapping herself around Bennett like a supplicant. He refused. He knew she couldn't handle it. He explained as sympathetically as he knew how that she was going to be taken into police custody. Things weren't nearly as grim as they appeared, he assured her. "It's not like on TV. You'll be put in a cell but we'll try to make it as comfortable as possible."

Bennett had spent 22 years on the force and thought he'd seen just about everything. As a corporal with the general investigative section, he'd probed plenty of murders, robberies, and sexual assaults. As a cop, he tried not to get too personally involved in these things. But this case was different, and he wasn't alone in his feelings.

Not since the 1982 shooting of Billy Stafford by Jane Hurshman in Bangs Falls had Nova Scotia police – or the public – felt so empathetic to a female killer. Hurshman, 33, blew out her common-law husband's brains with a shotgun after enduring a marriage of constant beatings, bizarre, painful sexual acts, and child abuse.

Like the Stafford killing, the Power affair sent shock waves up and down Nova Scotia. As snippets of information about Lisa MacDonald's oppressive existence began to circulate, the province geared itself up for a troubling trial and outpourings of outrage. "It's one of these cases where you hated like heck to prosecute her," Bennett said. "You shouldn't take a personal look at these things. But I felt nothing for him and most sympathetic to her."

MacDonald applied for representation through Halifax's legal aid system and was granted Joel Pink, a top criminal trial lawyer, as her counsel. Psychiatric assessments were also ordered on MacDonald, who was subsequently deemed fit to stand trial.

After being placed on remand at the Halifax County Correctional Centre, MacDonald complained of migraine headaches and chest pains. She often couldn't sleep and on the nights she could, she had bad dreams. It was agreed she would be better off released on bail. Upon her release, she worked as a cook and kitchen helper working 20 hours a week for $4 an hour at Burger King in nearby Sackville. Burger King manager Rob Cole described her as a good employee who did satisfactory work up until a month before her trial when she was late three or four times. She was well-liked by her co-workers and took direction well from her supervisors. On November 10, 1988, she received a leave of absence because of her pending court case.

The trial began on Monday, December 12, 1988 with a burst of excitement as jury selection got under way. After 10 men were asked to stand aside, the province ended up with its first all-woman Supreme Court jury – something that placed Joel Pink in a strategically favourable position over Crown attorney Alanna Murphy. While it's almost impossible to "read" a jury, the defence preferred a panel made up exclusively of women because they would likely see MacDonald's case from their own point of view, rather than a man's. Perhaps they would be more sympathetic to her in their deliberations.

Court was told by a pathologist that the knife which killed Phillip Power had penetrated the intraventricular septum – a piece of flesh dividing the right side of the heart, which pumps blood into the lungs, from the left side, which pumps blood into the body. The depth of the wound ran approximately 9 to 12 cm from the skin surface to the inside of the heart. The "Gourmet Collection" knife police recovered from the station wagon was consistent with the fatal wound, the pathologist said.

Betty MacDonald testified that one month before her estranged husband died, she wrote him a letter, which she gave to one of her other sisters, Marcella, to deliver to Power. Why did she write to him? "People had been telling me Phillip and Lisa's situation and I felt bad for them," she said. "I thought if I wrote him and told him that I didn't hold anything against either one of them and that it might help him get back on his feet."

Despite Power's betrayal, Betty MacDonald said she was by no means hostile toward him. Occassionally, she pitied the man whom she had loved and who was now on the skids. "Phil and Lisa were living partially on welfare and going around gathering stuff out of the garbage." Her younger sister was described as "very immature, potentially suicidal," someone who has "never learned how to deal with a crisis in her life."

Sadly, Betty confessed, the last time she saw Power was in the hospital, minutes after he had died. Nothing had been resolved. After that, she described how she went to the Halifax Police station to pick up his belongings, which included an incomplete letter addressed to her.

Dated September 23, 1987, it said:

Dear Betty:
   Well it has taken almost two years to sit down and write this letter. I don't really know what I am going to write but I hope it might help you some and I also hope it might help me.

This was the note that MacDonald had found while cleaning on October 11, along with Betty's unlisted number. Who knows what Power was going to write in that letter, or whether he would have finished it. What words could he have used to explain how he seduced her younger sister into a life of abuse and irresponsibility in the name of love?

Patricia MacDonald, a sister of Power's and no relation to the accused, described her brother as a "friendly, passive person." Always a compulsive gambler, she didn't know why he couldn't seem to find work after losing his union job at Canada Post.

Testifying on behalf of the defence, Dr. Edwin Rosenberg, a Halifax psychiatrist, said that he had assessed MacDonald in November 1988. He determined that, at the time of Power's killing, MacDonald developed a psychotic reaction or brief reactive psychosis, spurred by severe stress. "The behaviour is clearly psychotic and out of touch with reality," he said, adding that a person can recover from it within twenty-four hours. Had Power not bumped into MacDonald on the street that day, he would have been alive, Rosenberg said later in an interview. "Her plan was to get help. She ended up encountering him in the street and it may have rekindled all of the inconsistencies in their relationship."

Rosenberg said he emphathized with her situation and compared it to battered wife syndrome because "she couldn't extricate" herself from him. She fantasized about Power and built him in her own mind to be something he wasn't. "He was someone who preyed on an individual with no defences. While I didn't think he was Billy Jo Stafford, it was not an unreasonable comparison," he said.

What about the premenstrual syndrome (PMS) that Lisa MacDonald cited on the day of her arrest? Lisa MacDonald continued to believe PMS was an important factor in the stabbing but Pink did not. "The PMS was a red herring," he said. "This was a case of physical abuse and a dependent personality – she just couldn't leave him, she had no place to go." At the same time, two psychiatrists agreed under direct examination that premenstrual syndrome could aggravate MacDonald's existing psychiatric problems, including mixed personality disorders.

PMS starts after ovulation during a woman's menstrual cycle, usually about 10 days before the actual period starts. While many women feel "blue" just before periodicity, some experience wild mood swings, compounded by drastic changes in behaviour. These feelings usually end with the onset of menstruation. The symptoms of PMS have been compared to the misery of drug addiction withdrawal and, in some cases, it has been severe enough to be accepted by the courts as a "mitigating factor" in violent crimes committed by women. In 1987, for example, a London, Ontario woman stabbed her estranged husband during an argument over child support. She was given a suspended sentence and placed on three years probation after her lawyer argued that her extreme behaviour was partly due to premenstrual syndrome. The stabbing occurred the day before the woman's period started. While PMS has never been the primary defence in any crime in Canada at the time of this writing, the case of the London woman is one of the few in which it has been recognized as a mitigating factor.

While it was virtually a given that MacDonald wasn't a danger to society and was unlikely to try to kill again, the prosecution took a hard line. Crown attorney Alanna Murphy didn't buy Pink's argument that MacDonald didn't have an operational mind during the murder.

"There were too many things she did after. She had the presence of mind to do many things," she said, referring to her call for assistance on October 11 and the reference to premenstrual syndrome at the time of her arrest. Murphy, in fact, thought MacDonald was "rehearsed" for her trial appearance. "She wasn't so sympathetic. She had a lot of coaching," she said. "Her answers weren't spontaneous." But Bennett, the cop, believed her. "I felt she was a sympathetic and pathetic sort of person. It was quite sincere in the way she came across."

To buttress her attack, Murphy called Dr. Syed Akhtar, a forensic psychiatrist from Nova Scotia Hospital to the stand. After lengthy *voir dire* arguments, Akhtar was not able to testify on his evaluation of MacDonald, which had been ordered by Joel Pink during a 30-day remand, because it was confidential. Since Pink did not accept Akhtar's psychiatric opinion of MacDonald, he hired another psychiatrist, Dr. Rosenberg. However, the Crown called Akhtar to the stand and placed a hypothetical scenario before the jury.

Akhtar said MacDonald's case file revealed a woman who had been subjected to betrayals in past relationships and dealt with them with emotional outbursts. Such a woman was unable to handle stress, had an immature and dependent personality, flew off the handle easily, is destructive and self-destructive. Although such a woman suffered from a disease of the mind, she would not necessarily be insane, he said.

After six days of testimony, the all-woman jury retired to try to render a verdict. Following six hours of deliberation the jury rejected MacDonald's claims of insanity and premenstrual syndrome and convicted her of manslaughter in the death of Phillip Francis Power. It was a difficult verdict, leaving not only MacDonald in tears, but some jurors as well.

Before the trial Pink had offered to have MacDonald plead guilty to manslaughter. He made the same offer during the trial. Murphy would have none of it – she wanted MacDonald to go to trial on the second-degree murder charge.

On January 20, 1989, Lisa MacDonald appeared before Mr. Justice Hilroy Nathanson for sentencing. Asked if she had anything to say, MacDonald made a brief, anguished statement: "I want to tell you that for the last year and a half I've been through a lot of problems and a lot of feelings. I've been through a lot of questions from both myself and a lot of other people ... The hardest thing that I've been through is every day thinking about what's been lost ... and about what his family goes through ... Right now I'm trying to help myself until I get stronger and it comes strange to me that I can't help them [his family] either. All I can do at this point is tell you that I'm sorry. [sobbing] ... I am sorry. And if I could bring him back I would, but I can't. That's all."

In a victim impact statement read just before sentencing, Power's 72-year-old mother wrote that her son had a big heart. "While the verdict has to be respected, I would give hope that some consideration will be given to our loss of a dear brother and a beloved son who was never as far as we knew or know the type of person described." A sister wrote: "Mom has not come to grips with Phillip's death ... Mom was looking forward to this type of person coming back home to be with her. Unfortunately for her and for us this can never be now. Her loss and Phillip's loss of life are a heavy burden all of us continue to bear. Phillip died a violent death and although it is agonizing for me to deal with his death in this manner it bears no relationship, I am sure, to the agony Phillip was in at the time of his death."

With that, Lisa MacDonald was given a five-year prison term, a somewhat high sentence according to Pink, given the nature and circumstances of the offence. A leave to appeal in the Supreme Court of Nova Scotia was granted but the appeal itself was dismissed. The three appeal court justices wrote that the length of the sentence was "well within the range of sentences usually given for manslaughter of this kind."

MacDonald served some time in Kingston's prison for women and then was placed in an Elizabeth Fry Society lodging in Brampton, Ontario. She is currently living somewhere on the East Coast.

TEN

Killer for Hire

SUZANNE Gravel woke at six on January 12, 1988 and began her morning routine. A walk to the kitchen to put on the kettle, a wash-up, and then to her bedroom to get dressed for work as a supermarket cashier. Careful not to wake her mother, she turned on the livingroom television with the sound turned down and frequently glanced at the morning news while applying her makeup.

Shortly after 7 a.m. that Tuesday, she heard some pushing and shoving in the bathroom next door. Living in one-half of a one-storey brick duplex, Gravel shared a wall with her neighbours, Wilfred Gaudreault and Agathe Brochu, in the small northern Ontario town of Kapuskasing. The noise, as she put it, was "funny. It was like someone was pushing someone else and then I heard her scream. She screamed about two or three times and at the end of her screams she would say 'Wilfred.'"

Then it was quiet. Suzanne looked at the clock: it was

7:15. While it was too early to warm up her car, she decided to anyway. That way, she could get a look at her neighbour's home and satisfy herself nothing was wrong. As she walked down the drive, she noticed a light on in the kitchen, and a scruffy-looking man walking alongside the house with his hands in his pockets. Their eyes met and she froze.

The man, wearing a green jacket and a toque, turned his attention to a beat-up blue pick-up truck with a white cap driving slowly down the street. Gravel walked swiftly to her car, locked herself in the driver's side, then turned on the ignition. Her heart was pounding fiercely.

She took a good look at the truck. Oddly, its headlights weren't on, even though it was dark. Falling snow and slick, ice-topped streets made driving a hazard that minus 18 degree Celsius morning.

The man with the toque jumped into the truck. As it drove off, Suzanne darted into her house and locked the front door behind her. She frantically called Wilfred and Agathe's home but there was no answer. She dialed 911. It was now 7:19.

While relaying the information to the dispatcher, she heard a rap at her front door and someone yelling. She recognized the high-pitched voice as that of Agathe Brochu. She let Brochu in.

"Oh my God, Suzanne, oh my God," Agathe said in her strong French accent. Gravel asked Agathe what had happened. Agathe said something about trying "to hide in the closet," then the two women went next door.

Constable Steve Kozlovich of the Ontario Provincial Police (OPP) was called to the duplex at 133A Avenue Road. The first thing he noticed were two women speaking French to each other in the living room. The older one, Agathe Brochu, a heavyset woman of 55, kept saying "What's going on." Kozlovich then walked up two steps to the kitchen in the small, brick duplex and noticed a familiar face – it belonged to fellow officer, Jacques Thibeault, who was standing outside the bathroom, down the hall, looking pensive. "You better take a look at this," Thibeault told him.

Laying on the bathroom floor was an elderly man, wearing only a pair of maroon jockey underwear. What had been a bright, ordinary bathroom now resembled an abattoir. Blood was on the toilet roll, electric baseboard heater, toothbrush, the vanity doors, toilet, bathtub and wall. A pink, blood-soaked towel was swaddled under the victim's right side. At closer inspection, Kozlovich noticed a deep gash in the right abdomen. The contents were oozing out.

Kozlovich tried to get a pulse from the man's right leg. Although the body was still warm, he could find no signs of life. He turned the victim over on his back to see if he was breathing. Nothing. Not wanting to waste a minute, he called dispatcher Rachelle Dube at 7:32 a.m. and told her to notify Staff Sgt. Larry Beauchamp that "the Kap" had a homicide on the go.

Murder was a rare occurrence in this town of 11,378. A cold-weather testing centre for General Motors and Hyundai, the Kap was desolate and miserable enough to serve as a prisoner-of-war camp in the First World War. But if a killer ever stalked these environs, the townsfolk couldn't remember his – or her – name.

Incorporated in 1921, Kapuskasing was established as a station along the National Transcontinental Railway, a line linking Quebec City and Winnipeg, Man. One year later, it was incorporated into the Canadian National Railway system and housed "enemy alien" occupants, who developed what is now a federal experimental farm. After the war, the community's agricultural base was expanded by a government soldier resettlement program.

Located 500 km northwest of North Bay, the Kap is flanked by the Kapuskasing River, a word meaning "place where the river bends" in Cree. Since the 1920s, the Spruce Falls Power and Paper Co. has been the economic mainstay of the area, supplying half of its newsprint to *The New York Times*.

Back at 133A Avenue Road, Agathe Brochu looked at Kozlovich and asked twice if her common-law husband, Wilfred, was dead. Both times he said yes. Agathe, her blue eyes hard and glassy as marbles, let out a deep moan and leaned on Suzanne Gravel for support. There were no tears, however – a reaction Kozlovich thought odd. Thibeault then walked the pair back to Suzanne's home.

The Gaudreault murder prompted police to place roadblocks on the eastern and western entrances to the town. Officers also cordoned off the murder scene and began to collect evidence. The coroner was summoned to pronounce the body dead.

Three days later, a post-mortem examination conducted by a forensic pathologist revealed that Gaudreault, 62, had died from blood loss resulting from stab wounds to the chest and throat. There were 10 stab wounds in all: one in the pharynx that ended against the cervical spine, a deep, triangular cut on the left jugular vein, a third in the left chest below the nipple, followed by two more in the chest. A particularly bad gash was a 22-centimetre wound to the lower trunk, cutting the left kidney. A deep cut slightly below the ribcage caused part of the small bowel to gush out. Two other stab wounds were to the left shoulder and left upper arm. There was also a large cut to the middle of his left hand which was likely made when Gaudreault attempted to fend off his savage attacker. He had been getting ready to go to his job as a mechanic with the Town of Kapuskasing.

Wilfred Gaudreault's origins were decidedly humble. Born on July 24, 1925 in Cap Chat, Que., he quit school at age 13 to work with his father as a lumberman. In 1945, he moved to Kapukasing where he worked in the bush. Six years later, he married Rachelle Brochu, took a correspondence course in mechanics and obtained a Class A Licence. They had a daughter, Diane, and a son, Paul, and then separated 20 years after exchanging rings. Soon after, he took up with his sister-in-law, Agathe, going out with her for a few years before deciding to live common-law.

Although described as hardworking and something of

a perfectionist, Wilfred also was known to be a bad-tempered man when provoked, and sometimes even when he wasn't. Still, the man with greying, straight hair, and rather goofy smile was not a heavy drinker and tended to structure his life around the humdrum tasks of saving money, working, and watching television. He was an unlikely candidate for a homicide.

When a serious crime occurs, the OPP usually gets a senior officer from its headquarters in Toronto to organize the case. Detective Inspector Wayne Frechette got the call at 8:55 a.m. that January12. As an officer with more than 20 years experience, Frechette, 42, had seen his share of murders, robberies and sexual assaults. Tall, of large build, with wavy hair and penetrating blue eyes, he was a competent, no-nonsense officer whose "good ole country folk charm" could elicit confidences from virtually any individual.

At the same time, Frechette could be a tough interrogator, especially in cases where time was of the essence. While he believed in the saying "you get more bees with honey," he wasn't a pushover.

Frechette ordered teams of officers to go door-to-door for interviews, a dog handler to have the animal sniff for clues, and officers to check everyone leaving town through the roadblocks. Scan all the hotels, diners, service stations, donut shops for anyone suspicious. Scour the dumpsters and the landfill site for anything out of the ordinary. Go to the Greyhound bus stop and the train station to interview clerks who may have unwittingly sold the killer his ticket out of town. Check the mill for no-shows and talk to the security there to see if they noticed anything out of the ordinary, he told them. Send alerts throughout the province that a killer is on the loose. Get Agathe Brochu's clothing for examination and take her into protective custody, he ordered. If she asks any questions, just tell her police are worried the killer may strike her, too.

At 8:30 a.m. on the day of the Gaudreault murder a man, shivering from the cold, walked into Sportsland Plus in the business district of Kapuskasing. Jacques Guertin, the owner, looked at the man and immediately thought of his resemblance to David Copperfield, the famous magician. Only this man had lighter hair and he wasn't nearly as dapper. His jeans, torn at the bottom, had blotches of dirt on them.

Guertin approached the gentleman and asked if he could be of some assistance. The man said he was looking for a cheap Ski-Doo suit. Guertin pointed to a rack near the wall. The man looked at the rack, grabbed a suit and told Guertin he'd take it.

A good businessman, Guertin insisted that the customer try it on for a sure fit. The customer refused. Noting the owner's quizzical look, the man said he was shopping for his brother and knew his size. He held it up to his body and said it would do. He pulled out four $20 bills and paid for the suit. Guertin put the suit in a plastic yellow bag, then watched the customer walk out of his store.

The entire scenario seemed a little odd and Guertin couldn't help but wonder about his customer. He flipped on the radio and a newscaster interrupted the program

with a bulletin: a man had been stabbed to death on
Avenue Road. With his customer's strange behaviour in
mind, Guertin called up the OPP and mentioned that a
suspicious man had left his store minutes ago. Could this
be the man police were looking for?

The David Copperfield lookalike's next stop was the
Model City Mall where he purchased a pair of gloves at
People's Store, a Walkman, and winter boots. An hour
later, he picked up a pair of blue jeans and a sweater from
Kresge's. He next went to Dubien's Mens Wear where he
bought a blue down-filled jacket.

Wearing some of his buys and carrying others in plastic bags, he began to hitch-hike on Highway 11 going
east. A waitress at a Husky Self Service Centre noticed
the solitary figure walking on the roadway. He walked
into the centre and asked her to call a Bluebird taxi.
Aurele Carriere answered the call. The man jumped into
the front seat and told the cabbie to take him to Fauquier,
located about 45 km east of Kapuskasing.

It seemed a routine enough fare to Carriere. Little did
he know that a murderer had climbed into his front seat –
one who had a sudden craving for a McDonald's ham-
burger.

Carriere told his passenger there wasn't a McDonald's
nearby, but the Moonbeam would hustle up some of the
fattest, best burgers in the Kap. He pulled up his cab at
that restaurant east of Kapuskasing and the man went in.
A few minutes later he returned with his burger and a
coffee for Carriere. When they arrived at Fauquier, the
man said he might as well be dropped off at the Driftwood Truck Stop, located outside of town.

As they drove toward the truck stop, they noticed two police cars parked diagonally at the intersection of Highways 11 and 655, obstructing their path. The passenger asked why the cabbie was stopping. "The highway must be shut down because of the bad weather," Carriere replied.

An OPP officer got out of his car and walked up to the cab. It was 12:48 p.m. Carriere asked what the trouble was and the officer said they had set up a roadblock. They were checking everybody's I.D. Just routine stuff, he explained.

Carriere pulled out his driver's license and introduced himself. Constable R.A. Wilkie of the OPP's South Porcupine detachment looked at it then peered to get a closer look at the man beside Carriere. The passenger seemed nervous, twitchy as he handed Wilkie his Blue Cross hospital card.

The card spelled everything out. It said the bearer's name was Richard Boucher. Born on Aug. 13, 1954, he lived at 161 Pine St. N. in Timmins. Boucher offered that he no longer lived in Timmins but was now residing in Iroquois Falls.

Wilkie thought Boucher seemed nervous and asked him where he was coming from. He replied Hearst, which is about 80 km west of the Kap, and he was on his way to Iroquois Falls. Boucher explained that he originally had a ride in the Kap but lost it. Carriere backed up Boucher's story, saying he was told to drop his fare off at Driftwood Truck Stop. There, he would get a ride to Iroquois Falls, about 170 km southeast of the Kap.

Wilkie let the cab through the roadblock and watched

it pull into the truck stop restaurant. Thirty minutes later, still feeling a twinge of suspicion, he requested a "10-29" – a check to see if a particular individual is wanted for a criminal offence.

Boucher, apparently feeling he was in the clear, switched to a Cochrane taxi and continued until he arrived at the Silver Grille restaurant in Iroquois Falls. Later he discovered he had left behind a red bag from Dubien's Mens wear with a snowmobile suit in it and a Kresge's bag containing a sweater.

At about 12:50 p.m., a blue pick-up truck with a white cap was located on the property of Spruce Falls Power and Paper Co., about a half kilometre south of the store in Kapuskasing where Boucher had bought his snowmobile suit. Ron Caron, who worked at the mill, noticed the truck abandoned near an area commonly called the Horseshoe, a spot even the most experienced mill workers had a hard time negotiating.

He called the police, who impounded the 1977 GMC half-ton pick-up. A trace on the licence plate revealed that the truck belonged to one Fernand Boucher of 54 Southern Avenue in Timmins. Further probing found that the elder Boucher was dead but that his son, Richard Boucher, had passed through a roadblock near Fauquier earlier in the day.

A search found blood on the truck's inside door handle and control knobs. Laying on the front seat was a copy of the Timmins *Daily Press* newspaper dated January 11,

1988. What a clue! Whoever had been in the truck had been in Timmins the day before. And that person was likely Richard Boucher. The pieces, it seemed, were starting to fit.

Halfway between the murder scene and where the truck was found, someone found a pair of cowboy boots stained with blood consistent with that of Gaudreault. Later, on April 28, 1988, police interviewed the owner of the boots, Guy Gauthier, who was able to positively identify the boots because of an indentation in the right toe where his big toe had been shot off in an accident. Gauthier, an Ottawa resident, said he had loaned Richard Boucher the boots but never saw them again. He briefly lived with Boucher in Timmins and described his former roommate as a man with a fascination about wanting to murder people.

Agathe, a clerk at Northern Telephone, was still at the police station that January 12, wondering when she could go home. Wearing a blue house coat, slippers and undergarments, she was introduced to policewoman Valerie Jarvis. Brochu sounded weak but didn't appear to have been crying. She talked freely to the policewoman, who was there to keep an eye on her and supposedly act as moral support for the sorrowful widow.

"My mind is a blank," Agathe began in what was to be a full recounting of her life story. "I feel like this is all a dream. This isn't real. I ran to my neighbour's for help. I ran out into the snow and I heard her car running so I ran over the snowbank to her door and I banged on the door screaming at her to let me in. I guess she was on the phone to the police. I was so scared. I got up early at 6:30 to let Wilfred sleep. It's my day off. I went downstairs to fix the fire. It was cold in the house. I'd put on the kettle to make Wilfred's tea. I washed my hands when I came back upstairs."

"Wilfred had got up and was in the bathroom so I went to my bedroom to lie down 'til he was finished so I could go wash my face and do my hair. Then I heard a sound. Like the sound a wet towel makes when someone snaps it at you. I got up. I hid behind the door. The shower had stopped and I heard Wilfred scream. I saw shadows on the wall so I knew something was going on. I tried to get in the closet but my toaster oven was in there and I couldn't get the door open far enough so I hid behind the door. I waited till there was no more sound. I had to get out. I didn't know if there was still someone in the house. I went past the bathroom and the door was open like this," she said, spreading her hands about 16 cm apart.

"I could see blood on the vanity. I ran outside. I remember seeing two sets of prints in the snow. I ran to the neighbour. My feet were all wet. I'll probably get pneumonia from this. I was up to my knees in snow. My neighbours got me wool socks and dried my slippers."

Jarvis listened to the monologue attentively, nodding encouragingly, acting the perfect compassionate confidante.

At 3:15 p.m., Agathe complained of having a headache. Jarvis promptly got her two aspirin, a coffee, and then rubbed her back, trying to soothe Brochu's tension. "Why is it taking so long?" Agathe repeated. "Where's Wilfred now? Did they find out anything? Where did they set up the roadblocks?"

Agathe spoke of the emptiness she felt over the death of her beloved Wilfred and compared it to the loss of her fourth child. "I was five months pregnant and I just flushed him away. I didn't know if it was a boy or girl. I went to the doctor and when I dressed I had no more belly and I felt so empty."

"I never wanted any girls. I wanted four boys. My first husband and I said we'd get married and have four boys and then God gave me four, well, three. I don't know why I don't want girls. Maybe because of my sister. My sister is older than me and if she was here she'd be laughing or saying things to tear me apart. She's just like that. Mean. She always has something bad to say about Wilfred. I was a social director for the cadets in SSM [Sault Ste. Marie]. I loved that. The boys all called me Mom. I did so much for them. I never realized how much I did for them till I stopped. The girls were different, though. They pushed me out of the way. They weren't like the boys. It was no fun after there were girls."

Reminiscing, Agathe recalled the time she managed to get Wilfred and his only son, Paul, together after years of not talking. She said Wilfred's first wife, Rachelle, had poisoned the waters between the pair and insisted that he not communicate with his father. Wilfred responded by not visiting Paul and Rachelle in their home in Sudbury and it turned into a stalemate. Finally, Agathe told him they were going to visit them. "They were supposed to meet us at six but didn't come till 9 p.m. They were scared. But we stayed up all night talking. It was beautiful to see them together," she said. "I'm so glad I got Paul and Wilfred together before Wilfred died. I said I would. We had a wonderful Christmas together. Paul came up with his wife on the 23rd and they had to leave on the 24th but it was nice. Paul cried and cried on the phone when I called him."

Agathe compared their last six months of living together as a honeymoon. Seconds later she contradicted herself, saying ever since Paul, then 24, came back and visited Kapuskasing several months before the killing, Wilfred wouldn't take her anywhere. "He wouldn't even go uptown to pay for me a coffee or pay for him a coffee. Always he'd say 'we can make coffee at home.'"

Agathe again asked Jarvis why she was being kept. After all, she could round up her family and bring them home with her. Jarvis explained that Agathe was at the detachment for her own protection and she wanted to keep her from being hounded by reporters and nosey neighbours. Agathe seemed to accept that answer quite readily and started to talk of her relationship with her first husband.

Agathe was married to Arthur Brochu for 25 years in Kapuskasing and had three sons by him. But the relationship soured when she discovered he was having an affair. "One day his foreman called and asked if he could come in to work. I told his boss he'd already left for work. He hung up then. I'd pack his lunch. He came home the usual time and his lunch box had crumbs in it. The next

day I packed him a lunch and again his boss called to have
him come to work. It was like a slap in the face. He said,
'Don't you know that your husband is on a week's holidays?' I was so mad I didn't say anything to the boss. I
waited till my husband came home and told him his boss
had called."

Arthur explained unconvincingly he had been at work
but he made the call to his boss anyway. "I was on the
other line and the boss said, 'Maybe you can fool your
wife but you can't fool me.'"

When Agathe questioned Arthur over it, he denied
everything. She waited until January when the kids had
gone back to college and he was at work to have her
revenge . "I had the movers come between 8 a.m. and 12
and take all the furniture from our house and move it to a
warehouse." Agathe moved to her brother's, where she
became, well, reacquainted with Wilfred, her brother-
in-law.

Back at the detachment, Agathe was beginning to feel
agitated. As the clock struck seven, she asked again why
she was being kept when there was a perfectly good home
she could return to. "What takes them so long? I wish I
could cry. Boy when I break down I'm really going to cry.
It's all building up. A lump in my chest. Right behind my
eyes I feel it too."

Aware she hadn't shed a tear, Agathe said she didn't
know why she couldn't cry. It was unusual, she said,
describing herself as a cry-ass. "I cry when I get a letter
from my son before I even open it. Or when someone
comes to see me, I cry for joy to see them." Once again

she asked when police had set up the roadblocks. Had anybody been caught?

Seemingly upset, Agathe mentioned to Jarvis that the officer back at the house wouldn't let her see Wilfred. "I asked him if he was dead and he just looked at me. It wasn't until I asked the officer a second time and he said yes. I wanted to see him. I realize now that I was pushing to see him and the officer held me back. I wish I could just see him now. Dead or not, he's Wilfred, you know."

Agathe then told Jarvis that she reminded her of her daughter-in-law. "I know when I'll break down. When I see the kids. We talked a lot about what would happen if one of us died. Wilfred said Paul gets everything of his. I told Paul that. He gets all the guns and tools and everything. His daughter will get her mother's stuff when she dies."

Panicky, she said she didn't know what she would do with herself because she had never been alone before. "I'll have to find something to do with myself like maybe I'll take that correspondence course in business administration. That way if I can't sleep at night I can just get up and read or something."

In the meantime, officers continued to talk to relatives and friends to try to determine why anyone would want Wilfred dead. His most obnoxious trait, it seemed, was an obsessive stinginess. It was understandable, of course, that a man of humble beginnings would wish to count his pennies. However, Wilfred seemed to carry his frugality to an extreme.

One vision Suzanne Gravel found hard to shake over the years was that of the couple's silhouette in a blackened livingroom, the only light on being that of the television. One of Wilfred's many cost-cutting measures was having all the lights turned off while watching TV.

The only time the couple did leave the lights on was when they went on vacation. Late at night they would pack their car, turn some of the inside house lights on, and drive away to parts unknown. Gravel knew they were about to go on vacation because Wilfred and Agathe would talk of how they looked forward to a soft, warm bed upon their return. Since hotels cost money, the couple slept in their car. Too embarrassed to tell neighbours of their cheapness, they would complain that they had waited too long to make reservations and there was no accommodation available.

Wilfred's need to save extended to the water bill. One time, Wilfred asked Suzanne Gravel how much her monthly water bill was. She said $7. He complained that his was $10, even though Agathe bathed in the same water he did. Dissatisfied with his bill, he had the meter changed and placed a lock on it. He instructed Suzanne to make sure no one was tampering with it.

Perhaps no one knew Wilfred as well as Rachelle Brochu, who first met him in 1943 when she was only 12 and he was 18. Eight years later, they married. Wilfred was a man of regular habits – Rachelle could set her watch by his comings and goings from work – whose greatest pleasures were of the small, domestic variety. Wilfred liked control of his world and built himself a safe existence around a loving, responsible wife. He was a man who wasn't capable of great passions because he couldn't take emotional risks. He was as predictable as punching in a time-clock. Life with Wilfred was safe, secure and perfectly ordinary.

There was a period, though, when Wilfred was in a state of agitation. It was in their second year of marriage, in 1952. Rachelle asked him to go to a movie with her but he declined, citing a headache as the excuse. Rachelle decided to go alone. On the way back from the show, she noticed all the doors and windows were open in the house, something unusual for a man whose law was "lock the doors."

Rachelle started to wander through the house, looking for her husband. Unable to find him, she went upstairs to her neighbour's home in the duplex and asked if she knew where her husband was. The neighbour, Blanche Menard, said Wilfred was in the Brochu basement apartment.

With that, Rachelle went downstairs and sat in her rocker, trying to figure out what this all meant. "The next thing, I heard whispering coming from Agathe's door [in the basement where she lived]. The next thing I know Wilfred comes in and he's all surprised. He asked me what I was doing there. I told him that this is my home. I asked him where he was. He said he was at Agathe's."

What did Wilfred find so appealing about Agathe? For one thing, she was passionate in her lovemaking, at times all-consuming. More importantly, she genuinely wanted Wilfred Brochu. Not as a husband, mind you, not as a man who takes out the garbage and weeds the lawn, but as Wilfred the lover. This was something new for the normally plodding Wilfred. For a man who had known nothing more than the ordinary, he suddenly had something very extraordinary in his grip. A man who seemingly never took risks, it seemed he was finally ready to break out of his mold.

Agathe, it seemed, had a craving for diversified sex in the form of clandestine affairs. She was capable of bringing out the naughty in the nicest and seemingly most faithful of men. Agathe, although a strong, somewhat dowdy woman, oozed and smouldered sex.

Rachelle tried to slough off the affair as an indiscretion. Until now, she hadn't understood why Wilfred had told her never to let Agathe into their home. "Wilfred told me to lock the door right after he left and if I opened the door by mistake to let Agathe in, I would have to kick her in the belly and call the police." Oddly, Rachelle hadn't questioned why her husband didn't want the sisters-in-law to become too friendly. Now she knew why.

What concerned her more, though, were Wilfred's frequent fits of temper. In an argument, Wilfred would resort to throwing and breaking dishes – anything that was handy, turning the home into a warzone of broken china. Many of the arguments were over spending money.

Agathe's marriage hadn't been much better. She had married her first husband, Arthur, in 1952, when she was 19. They had their first child in 1960 and called him Danny. She had a second child named Gilles and a third son, in 1963, named Ronnie. The marriage was a fractious one, marked by affairs and at least three temporary separations and reunions.

When they separated for good, Arthur Brochu told police Agathe withdrew all $40,000 from their bank account and took all the furniture. He had literally been cleaned out.

Meanwhile, as officers continued to interview Brochu's family and friends, Detective Inspector Frechette was focusing his efforts on finding Richard Boucher. One of the first things he did was call up Boucher's criminal record. He discovered Boucher was not prone to murder. His only conviction was for drugs.

Reading Boucher's history, Frechette found Boucher had three brothers and one sister. On July 10, 1976, just a month before his 22nd birthday, he got married and later fathered two daughters, Tina and Lizanne. The Bouchers legally separated five years after marrying and subsequently divorced in 1987. In 1985, he began to live with a woman named Bonnie Sopchyshyn with whom he subsequently had a child. His only job seemed to involve working out of Rouyn, Que. where he provided exotic dancers for the local hotels. Police suspected this was merely a front for pushing drugs.

Frechette sent a crew of officers to Boucher's hometown of Timmins to see if the murder suspect was there. "Essentially we were going to make life miserable in the seedier bars for people," Frechette recalled. "The message was 'Boucher's in town, tell me where he is.'"

Soon word came through that Richard Boucher had booked a room for one week at the Tisdale Hotel. Police obtained a key for the room and opened the door. "We find some stuff, like bags, clothing, I.D., money, pop and chips but not him," Frechette said later. He ordered two officers, one armed with a shotgun, to stay there. A 16-hour wait ensued but the suspect did not show.

At the same time, police got a tip that Boucher was in room 204 at the Empire Hotel in Timmins. They were told he was a cokehead and carries a handgun. At first the police search of the hotel drew a blank. "There's a guy in the room shitting his pants but he's not Richard Boucher," Frechette recalled. "This guy says he doesn't know where Richard is."

After further "discussion," however, the man suddenly "remembered" where Boucher was, and pointed to the bed. The cops were perplexed. While there was a fully-made bed no one was on or under it. Again the man pointed, emphasizing that someone, was, in fact, *in* the bed.

Whipping up the mattress, police found Boucher laying inside a cleverly cut-out boxspring, injecting cocaine through the veins in his arm. He lunged at a policewoman and tried to jab her with the needle. He was quickly restrained, cautioned, charged with first-degree murder, and taken to jail in the nearby town of Haileybury.

It was an impressive arrest, but at the same time, police didn't have too much. Sure, they had some good physical evidence, they had a nervous cocaine user who had been driving his deceased father's truck. They had a statement from Agathe Brochu about an intruder who had broken into her home, stabbed Wilfred, and stolen some money from her purse. They even had the testimony of an officer who had pretended to be a friend of Boucher's and phoned Agathe. That conversation revealed that Agathe knew Boucher – knew him so well, in fact, that she told his "friend" she would consider helping defray his legal expenses. But as strong as this was, police needed someone to squawk. Who would that someone be?

Agathe Brochu was subsequently released from protective custody and allowed to go as she pleased because she hadn't as yet been charged with any crime. On January 15, three days after the murder, Wilfred's daughter, Diane Dufresne, 30, went to visit her step-mother. Agathe had just returned from the beauty parlour after having her hair done.

Agathe asked Diane if she had "found anything" and if police had asked her anything. Diane in turn asked Agathe who could have done such a thing to her father. "What can I say to you," Agathe replied, sounding calm and in control. She talked of how strong she was going to be, of her hopes that the "suspects" get caught.

Two days later, a man named Rick Sauvageau telephoned police in Kapuskasing to ask if there was a warrant out for his arrest. Police by this time had determined that Richard Boucher had come to Kapuskasing January 12 with another man and that this man likely was Sauvageau. "He knew we were looking for him and he knew we got a tip that he broke down in a bar in Timmins and he started crying about it," Frechette said. "We thought he could either go down for the count as an accessory or be a hell of a witness."

When Sauvageau got on the phone with Frechette, he told the detective: "Sooner or later you're going to get me." Frechette explained his options, then told him to "haul your ass in here and we'll chat." Frechette sent two of his officers to pick Sauvageau up in Timmins.

Once he arrived, Sauvageau explained that it all had happened "innocently" enough. He bumped into Boucher, a man he hardly knew, in Timmins. Boucher asked if he wanted to take a drive up to the Kap with him. En route, Boucher said he had to settle a score with a guy who owed him two grand. He was going to collect and punch him out if need be. They could do a few lines of cocaine and have a good time.

The pair made the 150-km drive early on the morning of January 12. They listened to the radio, did some cocaine, then pulled up in front of 133A Avenue Road in Kapuskasing. Boucher jumped out of the truck and went inside the house while Sauvageau waited. It was just before dawn.

After several minutes, Sauvageau decided to take a quick walk down the street, then return to the truck. The next thing he knew Boucher had jumped in the passenger side. Sauvageau started to drive. He glanced over at Boucher and noticed blood on his arm. Sauvageau asked him what had happened and Boucher replied: "I did him in, that's all."

At this point, Sauvageau panicked. With the truck

still moving, he jumped out screaming: "On my God, I don't need this bullshit!" Boucher quickly took the wheel and drove away. Sauvageau took a taxi to a restaurant, then headed to the bus depot where he bought a one-way ticket to Timmins.

Frechette was happy with this information. Police now had a good, solid witness to go on the stand. The next step involved Corporal J.P. Racine of Sudbury's OPP detachment. He was placed in a common area with Boucher in Haileybury jail to see what information he could elicit. Specifically the 25-year veteran was ordered to find out if there were more people involved in the murder. On February 17, 1988, he put on his "bummy clothes," and acted like a robber who had just been bagged.

That evening Boucher approached Racine and asked what he was doing time for. "They said it was for robbery with violence," Racine replied. Boucher walked over to his cell and grabbed a newspaper clipping. Racine looked at it. It said Boucher was in for murder.

"That's a heavy one," Racine said as he handed the clipping back. They yammered on, then Racine told Boucher if he was going to be "good at it," he needed a good, solid partner.

"I thought my partner was good and solid, but the fucking guy hallucinated on me," Boucher lashed out, then stomped back to his cell.

The next few days were largely uneventful. Then, on February 21, as Racine was playing cards with a con before retiring to his cot for an afternoon nap, Boucher walked over for a chat. Racine asked him how much he could make on a pound of hashish. Boucher said he didn't want to talk about it. Racine explained he was only curious. The pair proceeded to talk about drug prices until Boucher said he couldn't do any dealing inside a cell. Racine then asked if there was someone he could get rid of for him.

Boucher: There is one guy, I've never told anybody about this, not even my lawyer.

Racine: Who is it?

Boucher: His name is Rick Sauvageau. He's the guy who ratted on me, his name is on the papers.

Racine: Can he hurt you?

Boucher: He can get me life.

Racine: Was he a witness?

Boucher: I don't want to say too much, I don't want to tell you everything, but that's the guy I told you went hallucinating on me.

Sauvageau, Boucher said, could be found at the Albert Hotel, if Racine wanted to do the job of killing him.

Racine: Was he with you?

Boucher: I just went to help the guy, I didn't go to kill him. The fuckin' guy hallucinated on me, I thought he was solid, I could trust him.

The pair talked some more, then Boucher blurted out: "The fuckin' guy has a paper from the police that anything he says cannot be used against him in a court of law." Boucher wouldn't elaborate on anyone else's involvement in the matter. Later that day, as Racine was leaving, he walked by Boucher's cell and asked if it was worth killing Sauvageau. "Ya, just get rid of him and my problems are over," he replied.

Racine's job was done. Police had confessions of sorts from both Sauvageau and Boucher. Now all they had to do was show the connection between Agathe Brochu and Boucher. This wasn't too difficult.

As luck would have it, Northern Telephone just happened to be testing a new long-distance system that, in part, allowed employees to make free calls to the north. The company kept a record of all the telephone calls made by employees. Police found that Agathe had been making calls to a Richard Boucher at the residence of Angele Prevost in Timmins.

Prevost, 23, a part-time stripper, had lived with Boucher on and off for the past five years and had one child by him. At the time of the murder, she had been in St. Mary's Hospital in Timmins for exploratory surgery.

On the Wednesday after the killing, Angele was back at her home when the telephone rang. A husky-sounding woman speaking French was on the other line and she wanted to talk to Boucher in a "bad way." At first, Angele thought it was Boucher's mother but after the woman accused her of lying about her lover's whereabouts, she realized the caller was no relative. "Don't lie to me, tell me where he is and when he is going to be back," the woman screamed at Angele. The woman, whom police suspected was Agathe Brochu, refused to leave a message. She called again at midnight and hung up after she discovered Boucher wasn't home. The woman called again and told Angele to pass a message to Boucher: Tell him that Wilfred is "okay."

Why, police wondered, had Agathe Brochu wanted Wilfred dead? Was it boredom? Frustration? Or money?

Most likely it was a combination of the three. Together, the pair had about $80,000 in a joint bank account. For the past several years, however, Agathe had been either spending or putting that money elsewhere. One bankbook was falsified, police discovered. Using the typewriter at work, Agathe had inserted new bank balances, which deceptively showed Wilfred that the couple was saving nearly every penny.

Where did the money go? One recipient was Agathe's nephew, Raymond Ouimette, a palm reader, who said he'd find a killer for her for a few dollars.

On June 4, 1987, Agathe met him in the Kapuskasing Inn where she gave him $5,000 to hire someone to kill her husband. Ouimette went to Montreal where he spent the money over a period of several months. Later, he contacted his aunt to say the hitman he had contracted had split with the money.

Later that fall, Brochu sent Ouimette another $1,400 to purchase a silencer-equipped handgun. Again the nephew reneged. On November 15, she sent him $600 to pay for a return visit to the Kap. On December 10, they met and she offered him $10,000 to kill Gaudreault. Handing him a $2,800 deposit, she said he'd get the balance after the murder. Agathe saw no results. In fact, Ouimette used the money to attend all-night parties and discos in Montreal.

After hearing about the murder, Raymond Ouimette decided to forgo family loyalty and go to police with what he knew. At first, they didn't believe his tale. But after he volunteered to wear a bodypack in attempt to get his aunt to confess on tape, they knew he was serious.

Ouimette's timing proved perfect because there had been a bizarre twist of events. Almost a year after the murder, Boucher – the man police had worked on so hard to get a first-degree murder rap – hanged himself. A jail guard found him dangling from the cell bars of Hailey-bury Jail on January 6, 1989, a pair of socks wrapped around his neck. Scrawled on the back of a court judgment was a suicide note, in which Boucher denied killing Gaudreault. Scarcely anyone, except for Angele, his girlfriend, believed him. (A week earlier, he had been convicted on a charge of conspiring to traffic narcotics and sentenced to 21 months in jail.)

Needing to build a tougher case against Agathe Bro-chu, police took Raymond Ouimette up on his offer. He met her on January 17 at a plaza in Kapuskasing, wired for sound. Ouimette was scared. Much of their 77-minute conversation consisted of the cat-and-mouse game of who knew what was in the suicide note Boucher had left. Ouimette seemed nervous that he may be implicated in the note and asked Brochu if she told anyone that he had received money from her to hire a killer. She insisted she hadn't. He told his aunt that he was afraid of her and she asked him why.

Ouimette: There was five thousand dollars. Remember that? Then twice in Montreal you sent me some, some more. Then I come here and I didn't do nothing about it. I just took off. You're not mad at me for that? You forgive me for that?

Brochu: I'm not even thinking about it. Ah, the past is the past. You didn't do nothing and, ah, and I got fucked, ah, what do you want me to do about it? I mean, Raymond, if I would open my mouth and say a word about you, well, we're both going for life inside, aren't we?

Ouimette said he had been so worried about the killing that he tore up every piece of paper he owned because he didn't want to take any chances. "All I got left are the clothes on my back and that's it and I don't care."

Brochu said she had "enough fuckin' trouble" of her own. "I don't want nobody else in trouble. Stay clean with me and I'll stay clean with you."

Brochu: "What we did was wrong but I trusted you, I gave you the money 'cause you were supposed to do something for me and you didn't.

Ouimette: "Well then I'm sorry. If ever I can repay it to you I will.

Brochu: "The only thing you can repay me is by keeping your mouth shut and stay away.

Ouimette: "Oh that you got, okay.

Brochu: "Keep your fucking mouth shut and I'll keep mine shut.

There was only one person she wished ill upon. That person was Suzanne Larocque, her niece, who had set her up with Boucher in the first place. Larocque was expected to testify in court about Brochu's request for a killer. "Suzanne [Ouimette's sister] ... shouldn't have opened her fuckin' mouth. And you should fuckin' rub that into her." The same went for Suzanne's husband, Jean-Paul Larocque, whom she described as a "cock-sucking, lying bastard," apparently because he backed up his wife.

Suzanne Larocque had already told police how Agathe had been shopping for a killer. Suzanne and Jean-Paul Larocque owned a strip bar in Opastika, a town west of the Kap. In the fall of 1987, she took Agathe to a restaurant in Timmins where they met Richard Boucher. Suzanne asked Boucher if he could find some more dancers for her strip bar. And, by the way, did he know of anyone who might be willing to get rid of Agathe's husband?

On the drive back to Kapuskasing, Agathe told Suzanne that Boucher himself was going to help her. Later, as a "downpayment" for the hit, Agathe withdrew $500 from the bank and gave it to Suzanne to hand over to Boucher. Suzanne passed the cash over and scrawled Wilfred's address and name on a slip of paper.

Shortly thereafter, Suzanne felt a twinge of conscience. After 11 years of being together, the Larocques were finally expecting their first child, and Suzanne was afraid the stress of the situation might cause a miscarriage. Frantic, she sent her husband to talk to Agathe. When he came back, he told her Agathe had called it off. She could now rest. The events of January 12, 1988, however, made her realize she had let her guard down too soon …

Agathe Brochu's conversation with Raymond Ouimette, along with other developments in the case, gave police enough to charge her on March 16, 1988 with conspiring to have her niece, Suzanne, killed and with the first-degree murder of Gaudreault.

The trial began November 12, 1989 in Cochrane, near Kapuskasing. There were few surprises and no press coverage until the day of the verdict. A host of witnesses trudged into the courtroom to give their testimony. Amost all were damning of Agathe Brochu, the "consummate actress." She sobbed in the "right" places but one time even prosecutor Bruno Cavion caught her faking tears and pointed it out to the jury.

Why did Brochu want Gaudreault killed? "I think she reached a point in her life where she didn't want to live with this cheap, old man," Cavion said later. "The best thing [she could see] was to get him bumped off." As a man of predictable behaviour, Wilfred was an easy victim, someone whose death required little preparation.

Described by the Crown as a "cold-hearted, blue-eyed killer," Brochu was calm when the verdict was read out November 29, 1989. After 17 days of testimony and seven hours of jury deliberation, Brochu was convicted of first-degree murder.

Before Madam Justice Judith Oyen sentenced her, Brochu rose and said: "I am not guilty … I did not kill him." She was sentenced to life imprisonment with no chance of parole for 25 years. She waits for a decision on her appeal while serving her sentence in Kingston's Prison for Women.

The rest of her family, however, still have to live with the sordid tale. Agathe's niece, Suzanne Larocque, said in a recent interview that she's "gone through hell over this." If there was any way she could forget it, she would.

ELEVEN

A Very Righteous Lady

Every morning, without fail, Imogen Souliere would go to 8:15 mass at St. Gregory Roman Catholic Church in St. Clair Beach near Windsor, Ontario. There, she would pray for her family, for the things she had, for the things she didn't. For the most part, though, 48-year-old Imogen seemed to have it all. She had a dutiful husband, Denis, 50, a secluded, four-bedroom lakefront home in Russell Woods east of Windsor, a beautiful daughter, and two sons. There were memberships in golf and sailing clubs. Imogen herself had a good job in the city at Chrysler Canada where she worked as a nurse.

Despite all these apparent riches, Imogen Souliere was not an especially warm or happy person. It wasn't that she was cold. She was just reserved. Adopted as a child, she was eager to give her children all the things life had to offer. Church on Sunday, family dinners, and strong morals were of utmost importance. She was something of a perfectionist, and she expected a lot from her children. Although she had the best of intentions, Imogen could be hypercritical and picky.

She applied those same high standards of behaviour to herself. As Father Raymond Forton of St. Gregory's says, she was more than any parish priest could expect from a member of his congregation. While she was too private a person to participate in bake sales and other fundraisers, she was generous with her money and reliable in her attendance. Imogen Souliere's life, in short, seemed quiet, devotional, family-centered.

The Souliere home on Elmgrove Road was anything but quiet July 19, 1984 when several Windsor police officers and a coroner arrived at the front door with a search warrant. Imogen Souliere was stunned. The warrant gave police the right to dig up her yard. Denis Souliere came to the door and asked what all the trouble was about. Detective Murray Sinnott said police had received a tip that someone had buried a baby in the Souliere garden.

"I don't know a thing about it," Denis replied.

"Well," said the barrel-chested Sinnott, "we can get a backhoe and dig up your property and find it."

A report of a buried baby wasn't the kind of tip one expected in this neighbourhood, or even in this city. Referred to by outsiders as a "lunch-bucket" city, Windsor has a population of about 200,000 inhabitants, many of them employed in the factories of the Big Three automakers, Chrysler, General Motors and Ford. Called the City of Roses, it is situated at the southwestern tip of Ontario, joined to the United States by the Ambassador Bridge, which spans the Detroit River.

It's over this bridge, in Detroit, Michigan, where all the "crazy crimes" occur – or so the Canadians like to believe. Abandoned babies. Shootings in high-school cafeterias. Crack deaths. Parents killing their kids. Life is cheap over there. That's what separates America from Canada, Detroiters from Windsorites.

Of course, there are those who think there's something that separates residents of Russell Woods from other Windsorites. A drive through the area is testament enough. It is an unmistakably upper middle-class neighborhood, where expansive, well-manicured lawns undulate like green broadloom. In 1984, homes in Russell Woods ranged in price from a "modest" $120,000 to triple that price. Nearby woods and a tranquil, serene setting made it *the* place to live and die. The harshest sounds in the area were those of the birds and the wind whipping off nearby Lake St. Clair. The community was the perfect compromise – country living in the city. It was not a place police visited often.

Shortly after 9 a.m. on July 19, coroner Dr. William Borre and a police officer began to dig up the Soulieres' garden with tools borrowed from a neighbour. A rake and a red shovel belonging to the Soulieres was taken into evidence. As the digging began, Constable Robert Nichols stood nearby, ready to snap photographs, while Sinnott made notes of their observations. Other officers stood by at the scene, ready to assist in whatever way they could.

They dug near a Chinese elm, in a patch of freshly-turned soil. When they got down about two thirds of a metre, they began to carefully separate the black, soft earth by hand. Within ten minutes, they had a brown plastic bag in hand. Borre looked inside and found another bag, tied with a knot. The officers stood by uneasily, gripped by anxiety and hesitant anticipation. Borre untied the knot and looked inside.

Lying at the bottom of the plastic garbage bag was the fully developed body of a female infant, diapered in a blood-soaked, yellow tea towel fastened with two safety pins. Borre turned the baby over and looked for outward signs of violence. None were visible. Borre was overcome with emotion. "People all over are trying to adopt children and this one looks perfect," he said to Sinnott, who felt equally disturbed. "You wouldn't even do that with a pet you didn't want," Sinnott said.

Borre stuck his baby finger in the infant's mouth and under its tongue. There was no trace of blood. He put the baby back in the bag and handed it to Sinnott's boss, Staff Sergeant Glenn Stannard, who placed it in the police car. As Borre went inside the home to make a telephone call, Sinnott talked to the Soulieres' sons, Richard, 15, and Robert, 14. After that, Sinnott and Stannard searched the kitchen area, looking for anything that could be used as evidence later at the trial. They found a package of garbage bags, similar to the one used to bury the baby. They also had a tow truck remove one of the couple's cars, a Chrysler Aries, so the front seat could be inspected for possible blood stains.

It was now 9:44 a.m. and another police officer, under instruction by Stannard, was digging a second hole, about three metres west of the first hole, except this one was behind a two-metre cedar tree. In that hole he discovered a green plastic bag, placed in a shoe bag, which, in turn, was covered in a black plastic bag. Inside were a piece of umbilical cord, some afterbirth, and two bloodsoaked sanitary napkins.

The baby and placenta were taken to the morgue at Windsor Western Hospital where Dr. Marvin Oxley, a pathologist, and his assistant, Edward Cribbage, went to work. They cut open the garbage bag and weighed the infant. She was 3050 g, just under 3 kg. Officers took photographs of the baby girl, who looked like she was peacefully sleeping on the sterile, steel slab of the morgue. Her height was 44 cm; hair: short, dark; and eyes: blue. A film found on most newborns, called vernex, was still caked on the infant, a sign that she hadn't been washed. She also hadn't been fed. There was no decomposition or rigor mortis. Other than what appeared to be fingernail marks on the infant's neck and nose, it was a healthy baby. The cause of death was precise: asphyxiation due to manual strangulation (homicidal). Oxley determined someone had strangled her just under the jaw, while pinching her nose. The lungs had air in them, meaning that the baby had been alive at birth and did breathe.

As a result of the post-mortem report, Imogen Souliere was charged with first-degree murder. In addition, both she and her husband were charged with unlawfully concealing a dead body. On Friday, July 20 – her birthday – Imogen was remanded to Windsor Jail while her husband was released on a $20,000 personal recognizance bond.

The incident shocked Windsor. A sordid tale that

seemed more "at home" across the river in Detroit was now unfolding in pleasant, law-abiding Canada. *Windsor Star* police reporter Jim Potter interviewed some of the Soulieres' neighbours. They told him that when police first arrived at the Souliere home, they thought the officers were responding to a break-in. They couldn't believe a baby had been buried near the shrubs. The Soulieres, after all, were upstanding citizens, people who had never shown disrespect to anyone in the ten years they'd lived in Russell Woods. They were proper people, concerned about doing the right thing. Imogen was described as a "well-educated, articulate, well put-together woman." A nurse for twenty-nine years, Imogen had spent much of her time in the maternity ward and delivery room. She had even done a stint as head nurse of the seventh floor of the Hôtel Dieu hospital in downtown Windsor. In 1970, after fourteen years in hospitals, she joined Chrysler as a nurse in its Windsor plant.

Perhaps the person most shocked in Russell Woods was elderly Father Forton. While it's true Imogen wasn't the most outgoing woman, he confessed she was "one of the nicest persons I've ever met." Only one year before the tragedy, he had given Imogen and her husband "a very beautiful scroll" with the signature of the Holy Father (Pope John Paul II) to commemorate their twenty-fifth wedding anniversary. The document had a picture of the Pope and the date of their wedding – June 7, 1958. "It was a beautiful ceremony," he said.

As much as Forton realized the Souliere family needed him in that time of distress, he had a difficult time facing them at first. "I'm very sentimental – I cry over the least little thing."

Soon, Russell Woods was swarmed by the nosey, the curious and the ghoulish who would drive out to Elmgrove Road to cruise the neighborhood and see where the infant had been buried. Windsorites picked "sides," argued theories. Tasteless "garden tips" began to circulate. An American tabloid dubbed Imogen the "Grim Reaper Granny." Soon people divided into two camps: there were those who believed she did it because she was charged, and those who believed she didn't because she was too good a person. Imogen Souliere, after all, was a devout Catholic, undoubtedly "pro-life" on such issues as abortion and euthanasia. Not only that, the Soulieres had adopted their eldest son through the Roman Catholic Children's Aid Society after doctors deemed it unwise for Imogen to try to bear more children. And in the mid-seventies she had had an addition built on to their Russell Woods home to accommodate her ailing, widowed father. A baby-killer? It just didn't seem to make any sense. Still, they wondered, how *had* Imogen Souliere made such a mess of her previously well-ordered life?

The unravelling began at about 2:30 a.m. on July 17, 1984, when 19-year-old Renee Marie Souliere, a second-year psychology student at the University of Windsor, stumbled into the apartment bathroom of her friend, Bonnie Johnson.

Souliere did not live with Johnson, whom she had first met at university in 1983. Rather, she used her friend's downtown apartment as a place to "crash" on weekends, using some of the income she made from a part-time supermarket job to buy groceries for Johnson as payment.

The oldest child of Denis and Imogen Souliere, Renee was tall, raven-haired, beautiful. This morning, however, Renee was suffering from vaginal bleeding and acute abdominal pain. As the hours passed in her friend's bathroom, the pain steadily increased. Finally at 6:30 a.m., she couldn't stand it any longer. She called to Johnson. "Please phone my mother right away. Tell her it's an emergency. Hurry."

Thirty minutes later, Imogen Souliere pulled up to the apartment in her Chrysler Aries.

"Renee you're pregnant!"

"No, I'm not," Renee snapped.

"Yes you are!"

Realizing she could no longer lie, Renee acknowledged the truth. "I'm sorry mom. I didn't know." Bonnie Johnson also had no idea her friend was pregnant.

Placing Renee on the couch, Imogen Souliere quickly determined that her daughter was about to give birth. She asked for something with which to break the water. Johnson handed her a butcher knife. After that, "everything appeared to gush out like a fountain," Johnson said. The baby girl slid out "like a greased salami." The umbilical cord was cut with scissors, then tied with a shoelace.

As soon as the baby was out of the womb, she began to cry. Imogen asked: "Can anyone hear that?" Johnson cuddled the baby and let her suck her finger as she took the infant into the kitchen and made a diaper from a tea towel.

After a brief talk, mother and daughter decided it would be best if the newborn was put up for adoption. Imogen asked Johnson to check for birthmarks, just in case Renee might wish to search for her daughter later in life.

Imogen tried twice to contact a doctor she knew but the line was busy. She dismissed the idea of going to the two hospitals that were closest – Metropolitan and Hôtel Dieu – because she knew people there and she didn't want Renee to "get a name." Eventually, Imogen placed the baby into the car, with the intention of taking it downtown to Salvation Army Grace Hospital, while an exhausted Renee stayed in the apartment, bleeding.

About ninety minutes later, Bonnie Johnson received a call from the new grandmother saying that, while en route to the hospital, the poor infant had died in the front seat of her car. The baby had been making "suckling" noises and then blood had come out of its mouth. Despite efforts to resuscitate the baby, it aspirated and died. "Bonnie, you should have come with me," Imogen told Johnson. "The most terrible thing has happened. I feel like such a murderer,"

She went on to say that she had been so non-plussed by the death that she drove home with the infant and placed it in a laundry basket in her bedroom. Once Denis got home and the boys had fallen asleep, she told John-son, the baby would be buried in the backyard.

Meanwhile, Renee Souliere wasn't doing so well. Sore, exhausted, frightened, she continued to bleed pro-fusely. Imogen told Johnson she would visit later in the evening as there was a funeral of her husband's aunt she had to attend during the day.

Bonnie Johnson liked and admired her friend's mother. She always seemed to know the right thing to do. And there was no reason to doubt her story about the baby's death. But still, she wondered, was burying a baby in a backyard proper? Shouldn't there be a funeral? The baby had been a real person, if only for a few hours. A respectful burial was the right thing to do. After briefly discussing the matter with a friend, Johnson decided to phone the Windsor Police. Maybe they could see that the poor infant got a proper exit from this world.

When the trial of Imogen Souliere began on Sep-tember 30, 1985, friends – many of them registered nurses – crammed into the courtroom. Some testified in her defence, which was led by a former judge, Thomas Docherty. Huron County Crown prosecutor Bob Morris acted for the prosecution while Mr. Justice Elmer Smith of Toronto presided over the eight-woman, four-man jury.

Father Raymond Forton was among the crowd. "I dis-believed it [the murder charge] right off the bat. She would never, ever kill anybody." The only thing that dis-turbed Forton, like others, were the circumstances of the baby's burial. Denis Souliere, after all, had freely admit-ted to burying the child in his garden.

Burying the baby was one thing, but why did the couple have another hole for the placenta? The explanation was simple. When Imogen returned to her Russell Woods home after visiting with Renee the night of the birth, her husband, Denis, told her it had "all been taken care of." While Imogen was out of the house, Denis went into the trunk of her car and removed a garbage bag – containing what he assumed was his granddaughter – then buried it in the garden. In fact, it was the placenta. When Imogen arrived, she discovered her husband had buried the wrong bag. "In the agony of the moment I simply dutifully prepared another site [for the infant]," Denis explained.

Among others, Forton could see that Renee's having a child out of wedlock was probably a "terrible shock" for her mother. Perhaps in Imogen's mind it would be a disgrace to the family name. But could Imogen, a woman who had spent her life helping the sick and dying, possibly kill her own blood? Definitely not. She thought too much of life. Adoption was the only alternative, not murder, her friends rationalized.

Crown attorney Robert Morris saw the situation differently. Souliere, he maintained, was a distant woman who cared very much about appearances. She couldn't live with the fact that her daughter had had a child out of wedlock. Zealously religious, Imogen Souliere was a woman with a low threshold for shame. She strangled the baby on the way to the hospital and tried to make it appear she died of natural causes.

During the trial, Morris would paint Souliere as an overbearing woman who "ruled the roost." Her husband,

Denis, simply did what she wanted, when she wanted. Imogen's relationship with her daughter was a distant one. She was an opinionated woman who was strict with her children and expected a lot, maybe even too much, from them.

Forty-eight exhibits were entered into evidence in all, including the scissors used to snip the infant's umbilical cord, the shoelace that was used to tied it off, the make-shift diaper, and fabric from the blood-stained front seat.

One of the first things Docherty objected to was admitting some of the baby photographs into evidence, arguing they were inflammatory.

One of the most eagerly-anticipated witnesses was Renee Marie Souliere. Now a fashionably dressed 21-year-old, she had since dropped out of university to work full-time. For the past 15 months, she had been the subject of much innuendo. Some said that her baby had been disposed of because its father was black – a claim that was patently untrue and irrelevant. Still, the identity of the father was never revealed in court. As a courtesy to the families, police destroyed all such evidence, and in the preliminary hearing he is referred to only as "Scott."

Renee told the jury that she kept her impending motherhood a secret because "I didn't want to be pregnant." She continued to live in her parents' home, her condition undetected by them, wearing loose-fitting clothing to hide her modest weight gain (by her eighth months of pregnancy she had gained only six kg). At no point did she seek pre-natal care from a physician.

After the delivery of the child, she said her mother

had asked why she hadn't confided in her. "She said she would have taken me to Chatham [Ontario] to have the baby. I could have given it up for adoption there and no one would have had to know."

Morris asked Renee: "Had you and your mother ever discussed what exactly happened to the baby? Has she ever told you what happened to this baby?"

"We've never discussed it in detail, no. She told me the baby aspirated and died."

"The baby aspirated and died. Did you ever feel any obligation to ask her what had happened to the baby?"

"I believe that. Mother would not lie to me. She never has before."

"So you're satisfied with that, that the baby aspirated and died?"

"I'm satisfied," she said.

Renee Souliere seemed eager to support her mother. In July 1984, she had told police, in a signed statement, that "my mother didn't want me to go to the hospital but she was going to take the baby to the hospital because she didn't want me to get a name. And she wanted to see if the baby could be given up for adoption."

Now, before a court, she said that after the delivery, "I just stayed [in Bonnie Johnson's apartment] and my mother suggested I go to the hospital. I refused and Bonnie…agreed with me. She said that by now there was no reason for me to go."

The prosecution seized on this. It wanted to show that Renee's mother had formed the intent to kill while at the Johnson apartment and planned to carry out the action

on her own in the car. It also was eager to demonstrate
Imogen's callousness: not only was she a baby-killer, she
also left her panicked daughter behind to continue bleeding on Bonnie Johnson's couch. During the birth, Johnson recalled Imogen said: "I hope the baby's born dead, it
would make things so much easier."

Under vigorous questioning from Morris, Renee
Souliere insisted that her mother had not shown her any
disregard. If there was a discrepancy between the statements, well, "at that time, I was under a great deal of
stress. I just had a child. I was very weak."

Also testifying for the defence, was Windsor psychiatrist Walter Yaworsky who said he saw Imogen three
times; on November 22 and December 13, 1984 and January 15, 1985.

Imogen, who was out on bail at the time, struck
Yaworsky as an intelligent woman, a professional with a
good career who had been stable all of her life. Past emergency situations at work were dealt with in a "cool and
appropriate manner." She had never suffered from mood
swings or depressions, nor had her children. Although
some would like to think of her as zealously religious, she
was never "over-scrupulous or over-obsessive or rigid in
any manner."

After delivering the infant, Yaworsky said, Imogen
was in a state of shock. Her anxiety level was increasing
and she became even more distraught after trying without success to reach her family physician. He concluded
she was in an amnesia-like state of altered consciousness
after the death of the child. "She became emotional and

involved. She couldn't separate herself from it and it left her vulnerable and over-flooded with panic."

He said she was obsessed with "what ifs." What if she had called an ambulance. If only she had driven to the hospital after the baby had died. If only she had called for help.

"Indeed throughout the three interviews, there was this feature of trying to undo, through thought, the chain of events that finally did occur in reality...And it's an attempt to almost wish that 'things had been different if only I had acted in other certain ways.' The guilt and the depression which she had was also related to that," he testified.

Imogen Souliere told Yaworsky that she remembered getting into the car with the infant wrapped in a blanket and later stopping for a train on Tecumseh Road. "The baby was breathing and all of a sudden it was in distress, a little bit of blood around the mouth," Souliere told Yaworsky. "She told me she had marked alarm; noticed the baby was in some respiratory distress, and did mouth to mouth resuscitation. Then she said, 'And the baby just died.'"

At that moment, "she felt frightened, terrified, and a wave of helplessness swept over her," he said. "When she was recounting these events to me she would obsessively repeat, 'Why I didn't keep going, I don't know why, it's sort of foggy after that.'"

Yaworsky said Souliere remembered turning her car on Tecumseh Road, but couldn't remember what road she took after. "Suddenly," she was in east Windsor, heading toward her home. She drove about 12 km in a state of mental fog, he said.

When she finally arrived home, she was in shock. "One of her sons was out front playing basketball and she took the baby and laid it in the laundry basket. She called her husband at work and he asked her also why she didn't keep on going to Grace Hospital, even though the baby was dead. She couldn't give a logical answer," Yaworsky testified.

Imogen then began to fret. She questioned why her daughter hadn't told her about the pregnancy. She wondered if there was something wrong in the way she had raised her.

In other emergencies, Yaworsky observed, Souliere's skills as a nurse would likely have helped her maintain composure. Here, however, "immediately on finding her daughter, whom she did not know was pregnant, right in the throes of delivering a child, there was this loss of this emotional or affective distance by which most professionals operate in dealing with a crisis. Here she became very emotional and involved, as we say she was 'ego involved,' this is something that she couldn't separate herself from."

Her panicked state of mind caused the "blurring of what would ordinarily be sound judgment in the past," he said, noting she failed to call an ambulance or go to the hospital after the baby died. Technically, the state of altered consciousness is referred to as a dissociative state. "In such a condition what would ordinarily be conscious directed activity, in this instance, say, her driving the car, becomes detached really from her normal stream of conscious awareness. So there is a detachment or slight splitting, if you will, almost of the behaviour from what one is thinking."

This state is not unlike cases of sleep-walking where a person is doing tasks but he or she isn't aware of it, Yaworsky said. Although Imogen called her husband and Johnson to tell them of the infant's death, she obviously was not fully appreciative of the situation. "For example, she became concerned about making dinner, or a meal. So if someone has a shock or a trauma, you usually would be reacting to this totally. You would not be concerned whether a meal is available for the children and so on. However, because the event was so overpowering, Imogen's attention focused on more mundane, ordinary matters."

Yaworsky told the court that he did not find any intention on Imogen's part to avoid detection. Even though she knew a dead child should go to a funeral parlour, the burial of the child was a form of trying to "clean up. As if, clean up something that had gone awry," he testified. "So I couldn't get from her in anyway, nor was it my opinion, that consciously she was attempted to avoid a detection in some manner, but rather that this was an aftermath, still, of the shock-like, fog-like state that she was going through which was impairing judgment."

During his sessions with Imogen, Yaworsky said he found Souliere to be a "caring and concerned, feeling person, who had a solid conscience formation, who was remorseful and even still puzzled by her behaviour following the death of the infant. She was not feeling any guilt about the death of the child because she did not feel that she was in any way responsible for its demise. She was filled with self-recrimination."

Yaworsky sounded persuasive to Souliere supporters. However, under cross-examination by Morris, Yaworsky acknowledged his findings were based solely on what Imogen had told him had occurred. He never received a summary of the case from another source and only made his decision on the information gleaned from Imogen. He further conceded that Imogen's amnesia-like state could just as likely have occurred because she was feeling guilty and wanted to avoid such feelings.

As compelling as Yaworsky's explanations may have been, there were medical facts the defence could not escape. Dr. Borre, the coroner, had determined the baby girl died of manual strangulation, as had Dr. Marvin Oxley. Their conclusion was backed up by Dr. Charles Smith, pediatric pathologist at Sick Children's Hospital in Toronto, and Dr. John Hillsdon-Smith, chief forensic pathologist for Ontario. One other finding supporting manual strangulation were the tiny hemorrhages, called petechiae hemmorhages, in both the baby's eyes and chest cage. Petechiae hemmorhages don't normally occur in a birth, except in cases when the infant's head is trapped in the birth canal and the baby cannot draw air into its lungs. Those instances occur only in cases of a breech birth, either feet or rump first.

Dr. Smith said he didn't think that the birth of Renee Souliere's baby involved a difficult or prolonged labour.

Looking in the nose, mouth, pharynx, tongue and stomach for blood, he could find nothing to substantiate Imogen's version of events.

Smith explained that an asphyxial death is one where body tissues lack oxygen. There are several different types of asphyxiation. Mechanical asphyxiation, which is what he believed occurred in this case, is when there is actual interference that prevents oxygen from reaching the tissues in the body. That can happen by smothering an infant, throttling him, or compressing the chest to prevent its expansion. "When we see them [petechiae hemmorhages] in the chest cage we can be confident that there has been some obstruction of the air entering into the lungs at some level from the nose down to the trachea, down to the windpipe," Smith testified.

"I would have loved dearly to have found some explanation that could be given to ascribe this baby's death due to natural causes," he said. "And I simply could find nothing by which this baby's death could be explained from natural disease. This girl died because of an unnatural process. For an unnatural process it is going to be either homicide, suicide, or accident. And it's obviously not suicide. I have no evidence for accident."

The baby's death also could not have been caused by sudden infant death syndrome (SIDS), commonly called crib death, where an infant dies unexpectedly and a postmortem fails to identify the cause. In this case, Smith stressed, doctors had a cause. "This child did not die of SIDS. It doesn't fit the definition and it doesn't fit the autopsy findings. There were no congenital reasons to explain it. Congenital heart disease does not, for instance, cause death at several hours of age."

Smith went so far as to say the Souliere death entailed "the classic findings of a mechanical asphyxial death." The curvi-linear marks on the infant's neck were an "absolutely classic example of fingernail marks. In fact, I am at a loss to come up with anything else that could explain it. They are as good as, if not better than, an example that you could have hoped to see in a text book."

Even the way they are positioned on the neck is classic, he said. "It's very easy to obstruct the breathing in an infant. Infants are nose breathers, not mouth breathers. And so if you simply hold their mouth closed and obstruct their nose with your hand it's very easy to cause because they obviously cannot fight back and cannot resist that type of action."

Smith said death on television occurs much more quickly than in real life. Babies, in general, are "extremely resistant to asphyxia. A baby, in this situation, would not die with compression of the neck, or obstruction of the airway for fifteen seconds. And it would not die for thirty seconds. And would not die for a minute. We are talking several minutes. We are talking probably of more than several minutes in terms of the action that goes on because even though severe brain damage could be induced by a mechanical asphyxiation that lasted several minutes, that child would not be motionless at that point."

"This baby would have made sucking or gasping movements for many, many minutes. You know, it would not be inappropriate that this could have occurred for twenty or thirty minutes." And even after a baby has its oxygen cut off for 20 minutes, a doctor can easily get it breathing again, although it probably would suffer irreversible brain damage, Smith added. The Souliere baby "did not die in two minutes. And I can personally tell you – and maybe I shouldn't but I'll tell you anyway…Some months ago when my own son, after he was born and lived for several hours, when the decision was made, because of his malformations, to allow him to die, and his trachea filled up with fluid such that he couldn't breath, I gave up watching his gasping…after twenty-five minutes. So he did not die in two or three minutes. And his brain had been severely damaged, irreversible damage, but he did not stop spontaneous motion in two or three minutes."

Even if Imogen's explanation could be believed, you never grab a baby's neck as she did to resuscitate, Smith said. Getting to a baby's neck is a rather difficult process, and the only reason you would do so would be to feel a pulse, even though that is not the best place to get such a reading. "There would be no reason to touch the neck in resuscitation. And, of course, you would never touch it in this fashion. And there is no reason ever to try and pinch off the nose in a baby as you would in an adult," he stated.

Docherty countered Smith's damaging conclusions by calling his own coterie of pathologists and doctors. Dr. Eugene Perrin, a pediatric pathologist from Detroit, stated: "It was unlikely from the evidence that I have seen that manual strangulation is the most likely cause."

Another of the doctors called was Werner Spitz, chief

medical examiner for Wayne County in Detroit. Spitz said he didn't feel the crescent-shaped marks in the neck of the Souliere baby indicated manual strangulation. Morris, however, undermined Spitz's credibility by quoting from a book authored by Spitz and used by many in the field. It read: "The hallmark of manual strangulation is fingernail marks on the neck of the victim, though their absence does not preclude throttling."

Still, defence doctors' insisted that they could not positively determine how the baby had died and suggested the crescent-shaped fingernail marks could have been placed there during the delivery. A nurse friend of Imogen, June Beer, who specialized in the care of newborns, testified that babies can have "mucous defects." She was sure a baby with such problems would eventually die if not treated. Docherty tried to tie Beer's testimony with Bonnie Johnson's observation that the infant had had a stuffy nose at the time of her birth.

Ironically, it was during this strong show of support from Imogen's friend in the medical profession that Robert Morris' wife, Sharon, gave birth to a baby girl. "I went with her on [October 6] to Metropolitan Hospital. The nurses on that floor were split with their support on Imogen. It was an unnerving feeling to have people look at you. It just seemed awkward."

"Once my own baby was born, it just made this whole thing that much sadder," he said. "Once you're a parent, you tend to be even more sensitive to that issue."

A few days later, Imogen Souliere took the stand in her own defence. Speaking with emotion, she led the jurors through the events of that hot July morning in 1984. When Bonnie Johnson phoned to say her daughter was in severe pain, Imogen first thought that Renee might be having menstrual problems. When she arrived at Johnson's apartment, she saw her daughter on the toilet, bearing down.

Holding a colour photograph of her dead granddaughter, Imogen showed the jury where she had placed her hands on the baby as she delivered it. She insisted it was born face up, contrary to Johnson who said it was born face down. Imogen said she placed her right hand under the right armpit and left hand at the neck as she rotated the baby's head and slipped the shoulder out of the womb. She rotated the baby, she said, so Renee wouldn't tear.

After the delivery, Imogen said she felt nauseated. She had a cup of tea, then sent Johnson to the store to purchase sanitary napkins for her daughter. By the time Johnson returned, Imogen's husband had called. She broke the news to him. Imogen then picked up the baby and started toward Grace Hospital. She didn't want to go to the closest one – Metropolitan Hospital – because she knew people there and she didn't want to talk to them.

She drove down Tecumseh Road to Crawford Avenue in downtown Windsor where her car was halted by a train at a railway crossing. While waiting, she noticed bloodied mucous seeping from the mouth of the baby, who was "very, very blue, almost black." Imogen grabbed the infant, pinched her nostrils and breathed into her mouth. She quickly realized this wasn't the way to resuscitate a baby so "I started breathing into the nose and mouth, turned it on its back and hit the back and then flipped it over, pushed on its chest with my thumbs and felt for a pulse." There was no response. By this time, the baby was black.

Not going to the hospital "haunts me still today," she confessed, adding that the experience "was like a nightmare had just happened." As she spoke, tears welled in the eyes of her husband, daughter and two sons. Asked if she recalled saying to Johnson: "You should have come, I feel like such a murderer," Imogen answered, "I could have said anything. I was upset."

Under cross-examination, Imogen denied concealing the infant, adding that if she really wanted to hide the baby she could have dumped it in the lake. In fact, it was Bonnie Johnson who suggested the baby be buried away from Windsor so the dogs and cats couldn't get at it — a claim Johnson denied. Morris wanted Imogen to account for the presence of the fingernail marks. She explained they could have occurred during the delivery or her attempts at artificial resuscitation.

Morris: I see. And how about human strangulation?
Imogen: No, I did not strangle that baby.
Morris: I take it you would deny, then, a plan that you formed in the apartment to deliberately — with the presence of mind to know what you are doing — to get rid of this particular problem on your own, in your own way and then dispose of the evidence at home?
Imogen: I did not kill that baby.

This protestation of innocence was the last time Imogen Souliere spoke in public. After three hours and thirty-seven minutes of deliberation, the jury on October 10 found her not guilty of first-degree murder but guilty of second-degree, a conviction carrying a sentence of life imprisonment, with no eligibility of parole for ten years. Upon hearing the verdict, Imogen Souliere stared at the floor and wept as did her sons and the dead baby's mother. Denis Souliere remained emotionless, staring straight ahead.

A month after the verdict, the creation of the Imogen Souliere Fund was advertised in the *Windsor Star*. The ad read "If you believe that Imogen Souliere has merit in her appeal and you wish to support her, a donation to her appeal fund would be appreciated...the Imogen Souliere Support Group."

The trial had depleted the family's savings and Imogen was said to have asked her husband to forgo an appeal because of the cost. But he didn't. He put their home up for sale – asking $197,500 – to help finance it. All appeals, however, were eventually dismissed.

On March 26, 1986, Denis himself pleaded guilty to concealing a dead body, and had the choice of paying a $2,000 fine, or spending 45 days in jail. He chose the fine. "He was a guy I felt sorry for," Morris said. "He was personable ... he was friendly, affable. The way he expressed it, he was following orders. I got the sense that she (Imogen Souliere) was the one who called the shots."

Today, Denis Souliere works at the University of Windsor and lives in surroundings more modest than

Russell Woods. He is probably comforted by the fact that Renee has gone on with her life and married. Imogen, meanwhile, is serving the balance of her sentence among the 200 inmates at Kingston's prison for women, a tough place for a baby killer to survive. There's a chapel at the prison and that's often where Imogen can be found. This time she is praying for all those things she doesn't have – her family and her freedom.

Hot titles from
M&S Paperbacks

SPY WARS
Espionage and Canada from Gouzenko to Glasnost
by J. L. Granatstein and David Stafford

The Cold War may be over but the "great game" of spy vs. spy will continue, say the authors of this "path-breaking popular history." "A fun read. Descriptions of the back-stabbing, blackmailing politics of spying are admirably well done." – *Quill and Quire*
0-7710-3511-X $7.50 8 pages b&w photos

CHANGELINGS
by Tom Marshall

Fans of *The Three Faces of Eve* and *The Shining* will enjoy this eerie, critically acclaimed novel about an estranged brother and sister, each of whom suffers from multiple personality disorder.
"Fascinating fiction, controlled, assured … " – *Windsor Star*
"A chilling yarn … difficult to put down." – *The Gazette* (Montreal)
0-7710-5661-3 $6.99

KICKING TOMORROW
by Daniel Richler

The remarkable debut novel from Canada's hottest new literary star. Four months on the national bestseller list.
"An exhilarating romp … It crackles with wit and insight." – *The Globe and Mail*
"A gutsy *Catcher in the Rye* for the nineties." – Susan Musgrave, CBC's *The Journal*
"Excellent … entertaining and ambitious." – *Calgary Herald*
0-7710-7470-0 $6.99

Hot titles from
M&S Paperbacks

AFTER MANY DAYS
Tales of Time Passed
by L. M. Montgomery; edited by Rea Wilmshurst

Eighteen newly discovered classics penned by the author of the immortal *Anne of Green Gables*, collected by the editor of *Akin to Anne* and *Along the Shore*.

0-7710-6171-4 $6.99

CONSPIRACY OF SILENCE
by Lisa Priest

The powerful, award-winning best-seller about racism, murder, and apathy in a Manitoba community. Basis of the acclaimed CBC-TV movie. From the author of *Women Who Killed: Stories of Canadian Female Murderers*.

0-7710-7152-3 $5.99 Photos

ELIZABETH
by Alexander Walker

The definitive biography of Hollywood's much-married biggest star, Elizabeth Taylor, by the acclaimed author of *Vivien*.
"Informative, thoughtful, and understanding." – *The Listener*

0-7710-8781-0 $7.99 32 pages b&w photos

THE JACAMAR NEST
by David Parry and Patrick Withrow

Someone is out to bring corporate America to its knees and ex-CIA-agent-turned-insurance-investigator Harry Bracken is determined to find out who. Provided, of course, he isn't shot or blown up first.
"A fast-moving terrorist story leavened with sophistication and wit." – *The New York Times*
"The action never stops and the authors have a nice way with dialogue." – *The Globe and Mail*

0-7710-6931-6 $6.99